Contents

Dedication

This book is dedicated to the memory of my Mum and Dad,
Leonora and Gordon Langtree, who would have been both surprised and
delighted at the publication of this book.

CHAPTER ONE

RE Today

An Overview

A class of Year 2 children have been exploring the story of the Prodigal Son and have used drama to act out some of its important features. One of the learning objectives is to help children think about jealousy (why was it that the elder brother could not cope with the younger brother's return?). The teacher ends the lesson with a reflective question: 'Who in the story, children, was the most disappointed?'

The answer from a beaming six-year-old is swift and decisive: 'The fatted calf!'

Later that term the same class are discussing a special person that they would really like to meet. 'Just imagine,' says the teacher, 'that outside the classroom door is someone you've always wanted to meet. Who would it be and what would you like to ask them?'

'I know who I'd like to meet,' says James, aged seven. 'He's very funny, often on television and a really good singer. Can you guess who it is?' After many guesses, all of which are woefully inaccurate, James' voice adopts an exaggerated tone: 'You must know him – it's Des O'Connor!' (Who would have thought that Des O'Connor retained street credibility with seven-year-olds in Poole!)

In another school the children have been exploring Solomon and the idea of wisdom though 'freeze-frames' (i.e. the children have been recreating a story or incident from the life of Solomon and then 'freezing' the action like a camera snapshot so that other children can ask questions). The class are now thinking about the famous story in 1 Kings 3 where Solomon had to judge which of two women was the real mother of a baby. The teacher asks the children, 'What would you have done if you had been Solomon?'

Answer: 'I'd have run off!'

The teacher, quickly recovering composure, tries another question: 'Solomon asked God for the gift of wisdom. If you could ask for a gift, what would it be?'

The answers are quick and memorable: 'A jet ski, a pony and a trip to Disney World!'

These stories illustrate both the joys and the frustrations of teaching RE.

T he purpose of this chapter is to look at the special nature of RE, its contribution to children's learning and its place in promoting a relevant, stimulating curriculum for the twenty-first century. The following three sections provide a brief guide to the RE journey of the last twenty to thirty years.

♦ Phase 1: The Biblical Approach

Some people may have fond memories of their own experiences of RE at school; some, like myself, may have very little recollection at all. If the intention of RE was to produce children who were well nurtured in the Christian faith, then it must rank as one of the most spectacular educational failures. The evidence, I would suggest, is the contrary of this. There are many children nowadays who have little or no contact with any religious tradition at all, including Christianity.

For a long time Religious Education was seen as the telling, learning and regurgitation of biblical stories. Researchers in the late fifties and sixties realized that on the very basic level of education – the retention of knowledge – children were spectacularly confused. We know that Jesus was a special child 'because he was found in a cot floating down the Nile'. Who was Noah's wife? 'Joan of Arc' of course. And what is it about the Christmas story which seems to make it ripe for mega confusion in pupils' minds? A teacher once described part of the Christmas story by writing the heading 'The Flight into Egypt' on the board then asked the children to draw a picture of Mary, Joseph and the baby Jesus leaving Bethlehem. Of course, most drew the aeroplane in which the family travelled, happy in the knowledge that the person flying it was no less than Pontius Pilate!

More recently a teacher doing some work about the Wise Men asked, 'How did they know where to find the stable?' The answer came back, 'That's easy, Miss, they went by boat.' When probed a little further about why he had made that response this youngster pointed out that it said in the story that the Wise Men 'were shipped in' (worshipped him). It is not surprising that children who have little or no contact with any religious tradition find the concept of worship a difficult one to grasp.

Of course, Bible stories can still play an important role in RE but there are other key elements in RE which also need to be carefully considered if children are to learn effectively.

♦ Phase 2: The 'Cook's Tour'

The next phase was an approach to Religious Education within which a particular theme or topic would be chosen then every conceivable angle from every religion would be looked at. If, for example, the topic were 'Buildings', mention would be made of several different kinds of church, mosque, gurdwara, synagogue, etc. This model failed because it was simply relying upon children learning facts about religion. It did not engage children by beginning with their own understanding of buildings. It did not say to them: 'What's a place that's special for you?' or 'When can you go there?' or 'When you are in a place which is special, what kinds of thoughts and feelings do you have?'

◆ Phase 3: Religious Education Today

We are now in a third phase of Religious Education in which there is a genuine consensus about the central purposes of RE in the curriculum. I used to say that Religious Education refreshes the parts that the National Curriculum will never reach. I would say now that Religious Education is the conscience of the curriculum. It's the opportunity that children still have to explore questions about themselves, about their relationships, about their environment and to explore the fundamental questions of meaning which human beings have had to grapple with since time began.

First of all, Religious Education has a distinctive but not unique contribution to make to children's spiritual development. In the busy, noisy, hectic lifestyles that many people, including our children, lead, where is the place for being still? Where is the opportunity to reflect on what it means to be me and all the distinctiveness of being a human being? I would argue that spiritual development is about helping children to reflect upon the people, places, stories, objects and experiences which make them a special individual person. Part of this spiritual development involves giving children the opportunity to explore big questions: How did life begin? What will happen when I die? Is there any point to life? Why is there suffering in the world? etc. In fact I would argue that young children have an almost innate capacity for reflection upon these spiritual questions which we, as adults, sometimes continue to struggle with.

The second strand of Religious Education is to help children explore the question 'What does it mean to be a Christian, a Sikh, a Muslim, a Jew, a Hindu, a Buddhist, etc.?' It would be very difficult to have an understanding of life in contemporary Britain without considering the impact socially, ethically and culturally that Christianity has had in shaping society. Moreover, Christianity continues to exert a considerable influence in the contemporary world. A recent report on RE and Collective Worship from Ofsted suggests that, sadly, much classroom teaching about Christianity is confined to a dull exposition of facts without really considering the impact of contemporary Christian belief and practice. Furthermore Ofsted have also identified that work undertaken on the other principal religions is patchy in content and does not enable pupils to make connections between people's beliefs and their resulting lifestyle. It is particularly within this area that RE can make a significant contribution to pupils' cultural development.

◆ Key Skills and Attitudes

While RE clearly has its own distinctive field of knowledge and understanding, it is far more than just enabling pupils to describe external features of religion. It is about pupils developing a range of skills and attitudes which will help them to fulfil the two objectives enshrined in the 1988 Education Reform Act:

• to prepare pupils for adult life;
• to promote their spiritual, moral, social, mental, cultural and physical development.

The skills and attitudes overleaf lie at the heart of effective RE. Jesus once said to his followers, 'A second commandment I give you, no less great than the first: love your

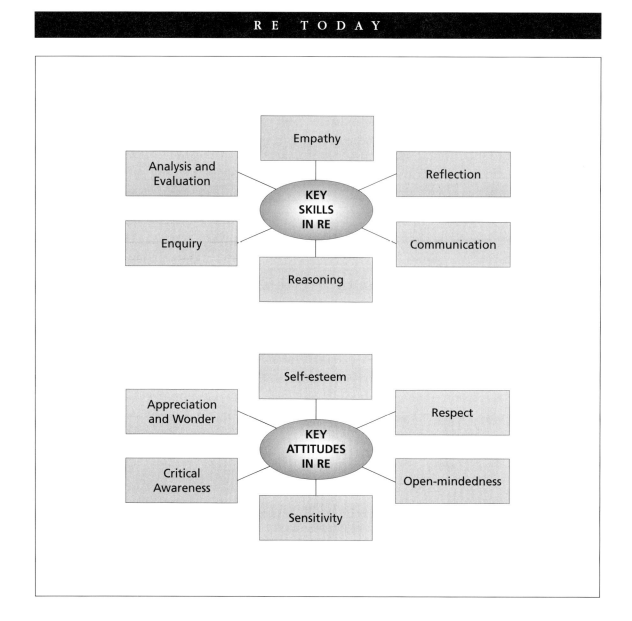

neighbour as yourself.' On this basis some children's neighbours are in for a hard time because some children have very low self-esteem. In RE all children should feel special, unique and valued simply because all of them have a spiritual capacity and a dignity as human beings that RE can supportively nurture.

◆ The Role of the Teacher

For years RE has been saddled with the notion that it is somehow a dubious educational activity in that it is indoctrinatory (i.e. putting forward one viewpoint as if no other exists). This impression has been highlighted by the fact that parents could (and still can) withdraw their children from RE and teachers could (and still can) withdraw from teaching it on the grounds of conscience. The very existence of a withdrawal clause can lead to the feeling that somehow RE is not as valid or worthwhile as other subjects.

RE today clearly sees the role of the teacher as that of educator: that is, helping children to explore a range of religious beliefs and practices and a variety of life experiences. It does *not* seek to persuade children towards (or away from) certain beliefs. By its very nature education is open and exploratory. It follows, therefore, that RE should be available to all children regardless of their faith background (and many pupils will come to school with little or no contact with any religious tradition). Of course teachers will want to be aware of children's family background in terms of religious belief when planning RE, but care and sensitivity need to be shown when encouraging children to share something of their own beliefs. Some children don't enjoy being seen as miniature role models for life as a member of a Buddhist, Christian, Hindu, Jewish, Muslim, Sikh or other faith community.

Regrettably, in the past RE co-ordinators were almost always appointed on the basis of their own faith stance – 'You go to church, you can look after RE!' – rather than whether they possessed the skills, attributes and knowledge necessary for the post.

Time to Think

1. How might your own beliefs influence your work on RE in the classroom?
2. What awareness do you have of the diversity of children's beliefs within your school?

♦ Objectives in RE Today

RE thinking and practice has moved on considerably in the past twenty to thirty years with a clear recognition that, far from being indoctrinatory, RE allows pupils to see the world from a variety of perspectives. The exploration of ultimate questions, the opportunity to consider the relationship between belief and action plus effective evaluation by pupils of their learning form an important basis for good contemporary practice in RE.

The key document in many schools will be their local Agreed Syllabus which sets out the requirements for RE in the various key stages. In England and Wales, RE remains in the slightly unusual situation of being part of the Basic Curriculum (i.e. it is compulsory in all key stages) but not part of the National Curriculum (i.e. there are no nationally prescribed programmes of study, statements of attainment, level descriptions, etc.). Some Agreed Syllabuses do use a National Curriculum format, others have chosen different approaches. The current legal position (based on the 1988 and 1992 Education Acts) is that any new Agreed Syllabus must 'reflect the fact that the religious traditions in Great Britain are in the main Christian while taking account of the teachings and practices of the other principal religions represented in Great Britain'. Agreed Syllabuses must also be reviewed every five years.

Most Agreed Syllabuses try to balance the study of Christianity with the study of the other principal religions (usually, Buddhism, Hinduism, Islam, Judaism and Sikhism) but also include material on exploring questions and values. The latter has sometimes been referred to as the 'implicit', as opposed to the 'explicit', dimension of RE. This is dealt with more fully in Chapter 2 (page 51).

The SCAA Model Syllabuses for RE published in 1994 (which are purely advisory and designed to help LEAs in the creation and development of their own Agreed Syllabuses) have two central attainment targets:

AT1 Learning about Religions
AT2 Learning from Religion

These two targets encapsulate some of the central objectives for RE today.

◆ Key Objectives

- To enable pupils to grow in their spiritual development through reflection on their thoughts, feelings and relationships.
- To explore a range of questions of meaning and how religious teachings have responded to these issues, e.g. How did life begin? Is there a God? What will happen when I die?
- To enable pupils to consider their own beliefs, values and commitments in the light of their exploration of Christianity and the other principal religions represented in Great Britain.
- To develop particular skills (reflection, empathy, communication, reasoning, enquiry, analysis and evaluation) and attitudes (respect, open-mindedness, self-esteem, sensitivity, critical awareness, appreciation and wonder) which enable effective learning to take place.
- To develop knowledge and understanding of both Christianity and the other principal religions represented in Great Britain.
- To develop an understanding of how religious belief can be expressed in a variety of ways, e.g. through art, music, drama.
- To develop pupils' ability to evaluate their learning experience in RE.

Time to Think

1. Which three of the above objectives do you consider to be the most significant?
2. How do these objectives compare with those for RE in your own school?
3. How has your school focused on the requirements of your local Agreed Syllabus or other relevant document?
4. How can RE in your school really engage children's interest and promote their spiritual, moral, social and cultural development?

CHAPTER TWO

Getting Started

Policy Statements and Schemes of Work

The previous chapter has focused on the nature and purpose of Religious Education within the curriculum. This chapter will consider how these key objectives, skills and attitudes can be translated into policy statements and classroom practice, and how detailed schemes of work (see pages 12–48) can support learning in RE. We shall also look at the important aspects of effective management and co-ordination of RE (see pages 49–50) and how a variety of 'themes and schemes' can help children become more-effective learners (see page 51).

♦ Policy Statements in RE

A good policy statement needs:

- To develop the full support of staff and governors (remembering that many staff may feel uneasy about teaching RE through concern over its aims and approaches).
- To bear in mind 'the ages, aptitudes and family background of the pupils in the school' (Education Reform Act 1988).
- To demonstrate awareness of the current aims and objectives which characterize RE. These include:

    (a) The contribution RE makes to pupils' spiritual, personal and social development.
    (b) Recognizing that in RE the role of the teacher is that of educator, i.e. helping pupils to explore a range of religious beliefs and practices and a variety of life experiences.
    (c) Helping pupils to consider their values and commitments and to develop a sensitivity to the values and commitments of others.
    (d) Developing pupils' knowledge and understanding of Christianity and the other principal religions represented in Great Britain.
    (e) Helping pupils to understand and consider different forms of religious expression, e.g. dance, drama, art, music, etc.

- To consider the skills which RE is concerned with (see page 4).
- To consider the development of positive attitudes which RE seeks to promote (see page 4).
- To give a brief statement about how RE is organized within the curriculum. This may include its contribution to topic and thematic work, its staffing and resourcing.
- To give some indication of the assessment arrangements for RE, recognizing the complexities of assessment within RE.

- To recognize the rights parents have regarding the withdrawal of children from RE (but pointing out the worthwhile and valuable contribution RE makes to children's learning).
- Future plans (short term and long term).

The key features for creating and developing a policy statement for RE are summarized below. The 'Deep Valley' example (opposite) shows one way in which a primary school might incorporate these features into their policy statement.

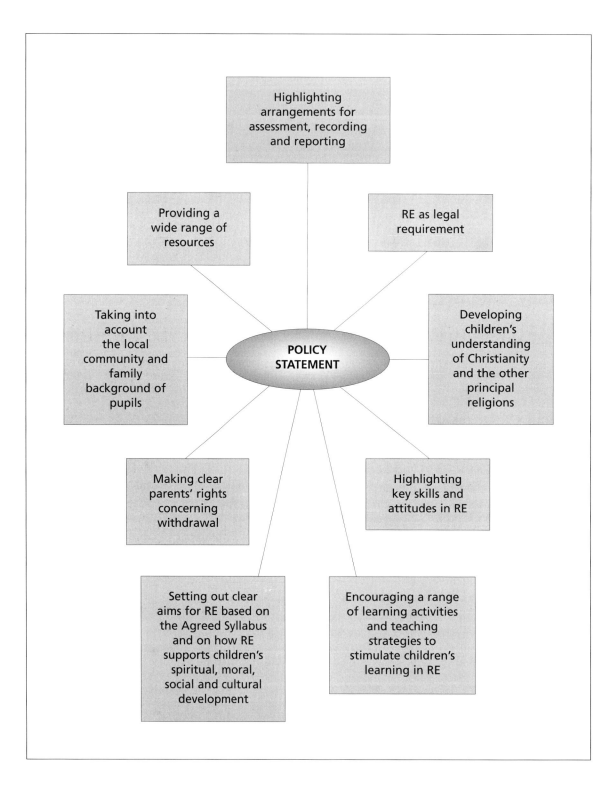

Draft Policy Statement

DEEP VALLEY PRIMARY SCHOOL
RELIGIOUS EDUCATION

At Deep Valley, Religious Education is delivered in line with the County Agreed Syllabus. The central aims of Religious Education in the school are to help children:

- Grow in their spiritual development through reflection on their feelings and relationships.
- Explore some important questions of meaning and consider how the world's religions have responded to them.
- Think about their beliefs and values in the light of the beliefs and values of others, including religious traditions and the values of the school community.
- Develop skills and attitudes which will support them in their personal, moral and social development.
- Develop knowledge and understanding of Christianity, its impact on our local community and its impact on society today.
- Develop knowledge and understanding of the other principal religions in Great Britain (in Key Stage 1 our main focus is on Judaism, in Key Stage 2 our main focus is on Islam).

Approaches to and Organization of Religious Education
We believe that Religious Education should be an exciting subject, so we employ a variety of teaching methods including art, music, dance and drama, the use of stillness and periods of quiet reflection, exploring artefacts, pictures and photographs, visiting local places of worship and talking with members of local faith communities. We also use story, video and food (a special favourite of the children!) to support our learning.

Religious Education in Deep Valley Primary is organized into a range of themes and topics which are outlined below:

	Autumn	Spring	Summer
Reception/Year 1	Myself	Journeys	Special Places
Year 2/3	Families	Special Stories	Our Community
Year 4/5	Leaders	The Environment	Celebrations
Year 6	Heroes	Life of Jesus	Islam Today

Assessment of children's learning follows the statements of attainment set out in the Agreed Syllabus. (Copies are available to parents on request.)

Skills and Abilities
At Deep Valley we believe that Religious Education has a major contribution to make to children's learning, especially in terms of their spiritual awareness. Important skills we seek to develop include reflection, empathy (to begin to understand another person's point of view), communication (through art and music as well as speaking and writing) and enquiry. Important attitudes include developing respect, sensitivity, open-mindedness and self-esteem. Much of the work in Religious Education begins with children's own experiences and emphasizes how special and unique they are.

Right of Withdrawal
Parents, of course, have the legal right to withdraw their children from Religious Education on the grounds of conscience. We strongly encourage parents to contact the Headteacher/Religious Education Co-ordinator if they have concerns and anxieties about the policy, provision and practice of Religious Education at Deep Valley.

Summary
We hope that Religious Education at Deep Valley is an exciting, relevant activity for our children to share in. We regard it as a particular area of the curriculum where values and school ethos 'come alive' in the classroom. We are aiming to help children develop respect and sensitivity for all people and to understand more of the importance of religion in today's world. Future plans for RE include provision of artefacts in Christianity, Judaism and Islam and the development of detailed schemes of work for all year-group topics.

Planning Schemes of Work in RE

As with any curriculum area, Religious Education has to be effectively planned, delivered, resourced and evaluated if it is to meet children's needs and interests. That is why schemes of work play such a key role in developing quality RE in schools. An effective scheme provides guidance for the school, its governors and staff on the aims, objectives, techniques and learning possibilities within RE.

Traditionally teachers have often planned in relation to school-identified themes and topics. This led in turn to a profusion of spider's webs as teachers creatively planned topics to cover every conceivable angle and aspect. Somehow the entire National Curriculum plus RE has been clearly identifiable within the topic, whether it be 'Water', 'Journeys', etc.

Partly as a result of the framework of the National Curriculum and also the rigours of an Ofsted inspection, planning in schools now focuses much more specifically on programmes of study within each subject area. This does not negate the values of overarching themes and topics but highlights the need for schemes of work to be clear in their focus and targets.

♦ Approaches to Planning in RE

The 'Worst Case' Scenario

This is where RE is planned 'as and when it arises' or 'all RE takes place in assembly'. The reality is that it may not arise at all and we certainly wouldn't expect all Science or English or History to be delivered through assembly. These 'vehicles' for RE never get started because they don't take the subject seriously and give no indication of what and how children are learning.

The 'Topic List' Approach

This is where RE is identified by a list of themes and topics, e.g. 'Myself', 'Community', 'Signs and Symbols'. While this is a step forward it does not serve the cause of RE effectively. This is because again there is no identification of what children are learning, how this relates to the Agreed Syllabus and how it might be assessed. The lists approach can also lead to RE being seen as a bolt-on activity, i.e. if the topic is 'Transport', let's do Noah's Ark. (In fact whatever the topic is – 'Light', 'Colour', 'Wood', 'Journeys' – it would appear that you can do Noah's Ark!) Noah's Ark is a fascinating story about punishment, promises, relationships and 'covenant'. In its essence it is not about forms of transport in times of heavy rain! Death by Noah's Ark needs to avoided if RE is to be more than: 'Let's find a religious story to fit in with our theme.'

Some topics and themes do naturally lend themselves to effective RE, but some clearly don't. If teachers avoid making tenuous connections between the topic/theme and RE then this can only be in the best interests of children and their learning.

The 'Developed' Approach

A scheme of work needs to provide guidance for all teachers on the *what, where, when, how* and *why* of RE. Detailed schemes of work usually demonstrate the attributes summarized in the diagram opposite.

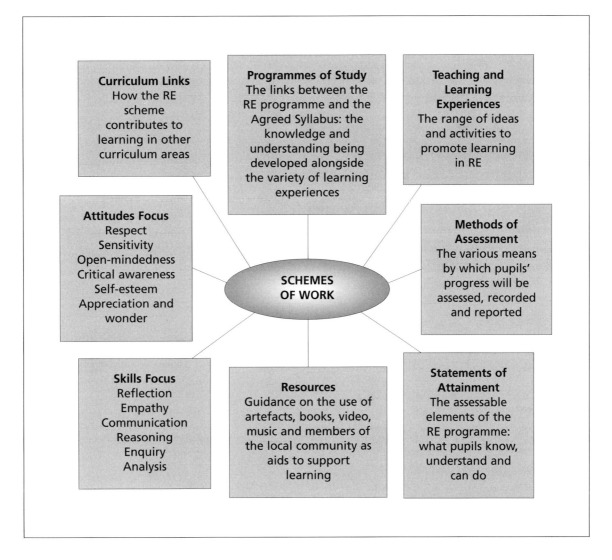

The schemes of work described on pages 12–48 illustrate three differing developed approaches to planning RE. For each model, a 'blank' planning form is provided plus detailed examples of how it might be used as the basis for specific units of work.

Model 1 (pages 12–26) focuses on planning learning outcomes and activities, highlighting key skills and attitudes. The worked examples, with support material, focus on the topics 'Myself' (pages 14–21) and 'Journeys' (pages 22–26).

Model 2 (pages 27–37) provides for the development of knowledge, skills, attitudes and concepts as well as giving guidance on teaching approaches and resource support. The worked examples focus on 'Celebrations' (pages 28–33) and 'Rules' (pages 34–37), both in general terms and through exploring the Jewish festival of Pesach (Passover) and the Ten Commandments.

Model 3 (pages 38–48) provides the greatest range of detail and highlights ideas for assessment, links with other curriculum areas and how a scheme of work can directly relate to Agreed Syllabus requirements. The worked examples focus on 'The Environment' (pages 40–44) and 'Easter' (pages 45–48). The latter is given both a Key Stage 1 and a Key Stage 2 framework, demonstrating how progression and continuity can be built into a recurring theme.

Module Title

Time Available

Form of Assessment

Intended Learning Outcomes
(What children should learn, experience, produce)

Possible Learning Activities

Skills Checklist
- ❑ Reflection
- ❑ Empathy
- ❑ Communication
- ❑ Analysis and evaluation
- ❑ Reasoning
- ❑ Enquiry

Attitudes Checklist
- ❑ Respect
- ❑ Open-mindedness
- ❑ Self-esteem
- ❑ Sensitivity
- ❑ Critical awareness
- ❑ Appreciation and wonder

Resources Required

Links with Other Curriculum Areas

Notes (e.g. tasks to be set, letters sent out)

Module Title MYSELF

Time Available Eight sessions of approximately one hour each

Form of Assessment Teacher's profile and simple self-assessment sheet
(see page 21)

Intended Learning Outcomes
(What children should learn, experience, produce)

* Considering the special people, places and objects in the children's lives
* Learning about some of the objects, places and people which are of importance in Christianity and other world religions
* Considering feelings about myself, where I belong, what I can do, what I am like

Possible Learning Activities

* Shield project: a range of learning activities which focuses on special people, stories, places, objects, friends and animals, developing an understanding of feelings *(see pages 16–20)*
* Beginning reflective activities to promote spiritual development *(see Chapter 5)*
* Handling artefacts
* Listening to and discussing important religious stories
* Visiting local place of worship to explore 'special' objects and symbols
* Inviting visitor into school to share their beliefs with the children

Skills Checklist
- ☑ Reflection
- ☑ Empathy
- ☑ Communication
- ❏ Analysis and evaluation
- ❏ Reasoning
- ❏ Enquiry

Attitudes Checklist
- ☑ Respect
- ❏ Open-mindedness
- ☑ Self-esteem
- ☑ Sensitivity
- ❏ Critical awareness
- ❏ Appreciation and wonder

Resources Required

* A3 shields *(see overleaf)*
* Artefacts from Christianity, Judaism, Islam
* Children's story Bible for key stories, e.g. Parables of Good Samaritan, Prodigal Son
* Candle and music for reflective activities
* Support materials for visit

Links with Other Curriculum Areas

Science and Health Education — my body

History — learning from artefacts, pictures and photographs

English — telling stories
— listening and responding to stories
— talking about experiences in and out of school
— responding to visual stimuli

Geography — observing places around them, identifying and naming familiar features in the local area

Science — understanding how living things are looked after and treating them with care and consideration

Notes (e.g. tasks to be set, letters sent out)

* Arrange for artefacts to be available
* Book time for visit
* Invite a member of a local faith community to come and talk with the children
* Let parents know details of planned visit and visitor

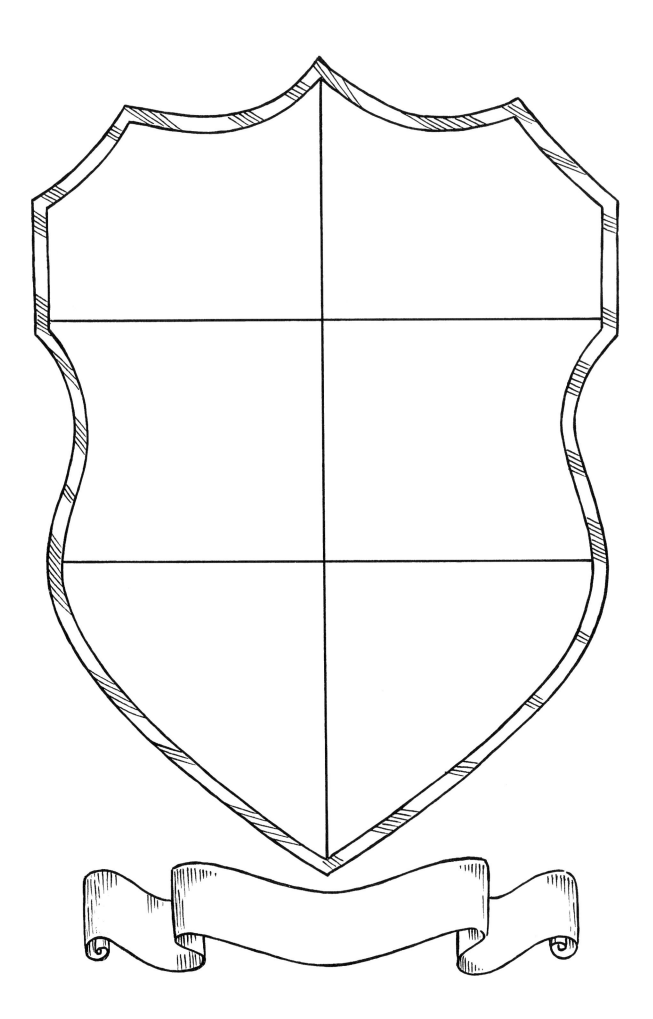

Myself: Shield Project

At the heart of good RE lies a commitment to the development of children's spiritual awareness. RE is particularly effective when it begins with children's own thoughts, feelings and experiences then explores the world of religion in terms of beliefs, practices and lifestyle. For many pupils who have little or no contact with any religious tradition at all, some key aspects of religion can, at first acquaintance, appear strange or even bizarre. However, if children have first been able to identify what is special for them in terms of people, places, objects and stories, then it is more likely that they will be able to perceive the 'specialness' of certain events, activities, objects and experiences within religion.

The following six learning activities are designed to promote children's self-esteem (a key attitude in developing good RE – see page 4). Collectively they enable all pupils to recognize their uniqueness as individuals and, when their responses are displayed, provide some really valuable discussion points on who and what is special for children. The activities can be tried in Key Stage 1 and repeated in Key Stage 2. (It is very interesting to note how children's responses change as they grow older.) The activities can be summarized on a grid in the form of a shield or teachers could choose their own design, e.g. a house with windows.

♦ Activity 1: Special Seasons

Children are invited to discuss thoughts, feelings and images related to the four seasons (e.g. summer = warm, beaches, light days). Within the classroom each wall represents one of the seasons and pupils are encouraged to stand by the wall which represents their favourite season. They are then asked to give reasons for choosing this season and within one section of the shield draw a simple illustration which relates to their choice.

Explicit RE Follow-up

Consideration could be given to how special festivals within religion relate to the seasons, e.g. Easter and the theme of new life. Opportunities also exist for exploring how stories can relate to seasons, e.g. the image of Narnia as a land 'where it is always winter but never Christmas' in C. S. Lewis' *The Lion, the Witch and the Wardrobe*.

♦ Activity 2: A Person I Would Like to Meet

Children are invited to imagine that outside the classroom door is someone they have always wanted to meet. Evidence suggests that children respond with an enormous range of people from family and friends through to Michael Jackson and Des O'Connor! Older children are asked to consider questions they would like to ask the person they have chosen. It is helpful at this point for teachers to encourage children to ask 'open' rather than 'closed' questions so that their chosen person would answer in more detail. Within the shield children could either draw a picture of whoever they would like to meet or identify the questions they would like to ask.

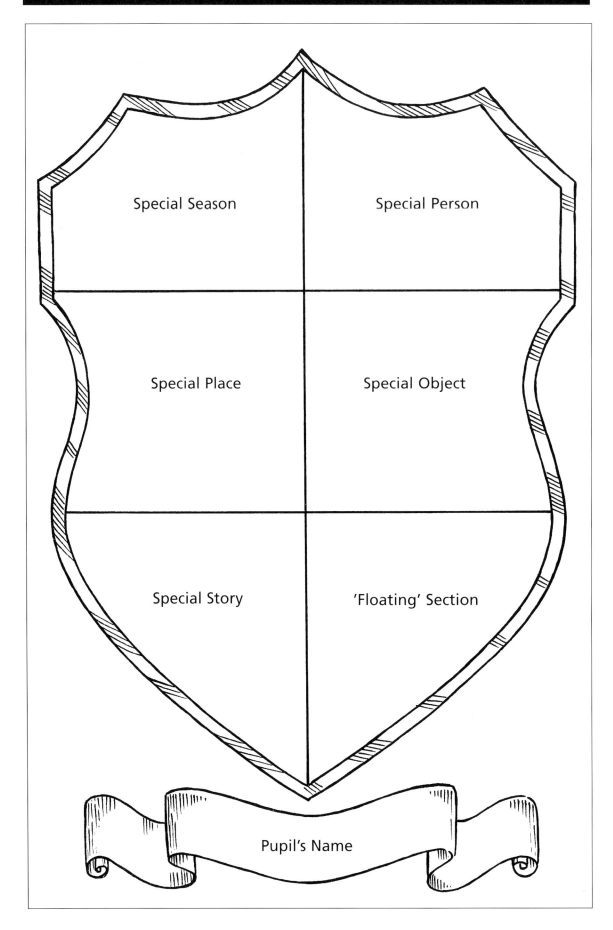

Special Season

Special Person

Special Place

Special Object

Special Story

'Floating' Section

Pupil's Name

Explicit RE Follow-up

Children could explore a figure within religion through questions, e.g. look at the life of Jesus through key questions such as:

- Why do some people today think Jesus is very special?
- What kinds of questions did people ask Jesus when he was alive on earth?
- What kinds of answers did he give?

◆ Activity 3: A Place I Would Like to See

In this activity the classroom represents a map of Great Britain. Children are asked to stand in the place (roughly speaking!) where they were born (hopefully not all have been born in the immediate vicinity of the school). Children who were born outside the UK are given a 'special' place within the classroom. Children are next invited to consider where they would choose if they could be anywhere at all in Britain. They then move within the classroom to where this place is (young children need a lot of help here!) and are invited to share where they are and why they chose this particular place.

Evidence suggests that the reasons adults give for what makes a place special (e.g. relationships, roots, outstanding natural beauty, a sense of 'getting away from it all') are mirrored in the choices children make:

'My special place is my back garden – it's where I feel the most peaceful.'

'My special place is where Grandad lives – we can talk and go for walks together.'

On the shield children are asked to draw a visual reminder of their special place.

Explicit RE Follow-up

Children could study a local place of worship and find out what makes it special for some people. Older children could begin to explore the concept of pilgrimage and 'life as a journey' with special moments.

◆ Activity 4: A Story I Like

Children are given the opportunity to share (through reading or telling) a story which is special for them. For older children the focus could be altered to 'a story that has helped me' or 'a story which made me think'. On the shield children are asked to draw a scene from their favourite story. Older children are encouraged to consider what elements make a 'good story'.

Explicit RE Follow-up

Children can encounter a range of stories from religious traditions and explore their purpose and variety of meanings.

♦ Activity 5: An Object Which Is Special to Me

Children are asked to think about three special objects which are important to them. They are then invited (within reason!) to bring in one of their objects and to talk about what makes it special. (Children have brought in an enormous variety of objects but gifts from grandparents seem to be of special significance, especially for Key Stage 1 children.) The primary focus here is on the development of respect and sensitivity no matter how repulsive the chosen object appears to be! Teachers need to show care and sensitivity in affirmimg the value of each object for each child, and to take reasonable precautions to ensure that treasured objects are not damaged or lost.

With older children time could be spent exploring the notion that not everything we value or regard as being precious is actually worth much in material terms. Children are then invited to draw their special objects.

Explicit RE Follow-up

Having reflected upon their own special objects children can engage in artefacts drawn from different religions. Artefacts are a vital and creative way of helping children explore the world of religious belief, practice and expression alongside demonstrating sensitivity and respect. Further advice about using artefacts in the classroom is contained on pages 84–91.

♦ Activity 6: (a) Floating Section or (b) A Person Special to Me

(a) A 'floating' section gives teachers an opportunity to relate their overall theme or topic to children's own choices, e.g. for a topic on animals children could draw their pets (or a pet they would like), for food their favourite foods and drinks, for transport their favourite form of travel.

(b) Using very simple aids (e.g. a candle with a reflective piece of music) children are invited to think about a special person for them (a friend or member of their family) and to imagine their special person smiling at them. Children are encouraged to consider what words they would use to describe their thoughts and feelings towards someone who is special for them. Appropriate music such as James Taylor's 'You've Got a Friend' could be played.

Children are then invited either to draw their special person or to write down positive words which describe that person.

♦ Conclusion

Once children have completed the shield, they need to be given an opportunity to pick out key features on it and to feel that they are 'special' because of the special people, places, objects, etc., they have identified. ALL the shields could be displayed as a focus for wider group and class discussion.

Draw or write in the boxes.

1. Three special things about me are:

2. Three special things I have found out about religion are:

3. Three things I would like to find out more about are:

Teacher's comment on child's knowledge and understanding

Module Title JOURNEYS

Time Available Ten x 1-hour sessions

Form of Assessment Simple self-assessment

Intended Learning Outcomes
(What children should learn, experience, produce)

* Enabling children to identify their own special places
* Enabling children to know about special places within religion, both places of worship (church, mosque, synagogue) and special journeys (Hajj, pilgrimage to Jerusalem)
* Helping children to identify key moments in their own lives (birth, special events and celebrations)
* Providing children with knowledge and understanding of birth ceremonies in religion

Possible Learning Activities

* Lifechart *(see overleaf)*
* Poem/illustration of children's favourite place
* Special places in religion: visit local places of worship
  (i)   Focus on symbols and feelings in Key Stage 1
  (ii) Focus on people and community in Key Stage 2
* Special moments in life: children bring in toys and clothes from their earlier years

Skills Checklist
❏ Reflection
☑ Empathy
☑ Communication
❏ Analysis and evaluation
❏ Reasoning
☑ Enquiry

Attitudes Checklist
☑ Respect
❏ Open-mindedness
❏ Self-esteem
☑ Sensitivity
❏ Critical awareness
❏ Appreciation and wonder

Resources Required

* Artefacts from Christianity and Islam
* Appropriate pictures and stories from Christianity and Islam
* Lifechart *(see overleaf)*
* Simple worksheet on Christian infant baptism *(see overleaf)*
* Simple worksheet on Islamic naming ceremony *(see page 26)*

Links with Other Curriculum Areas

English — speaking and listening
D & T — generating a design, judgements about familiar artefacts and environments
Art — use of shape, form and space in images and artefacts
Maths — graph work on lifechart

Notes (e.g. tasks to be set, letters sent out)

* Organize visits to places of worship
* Create display area for children's toys/clothes
* Arrange to borrow/purchase artefacts and pictures relating to infant baptism and Islamic naming ceremony

Some people think that life is like a journey. On our journey there are special moments. Sometimes these moments can be very happy and exciting (like having a party or getting something we really want). Sometimes they can be sad (like when a special person close to us dies or a friend moves away).

This chart shows one person's good times and bad times.
What might your chart be like?

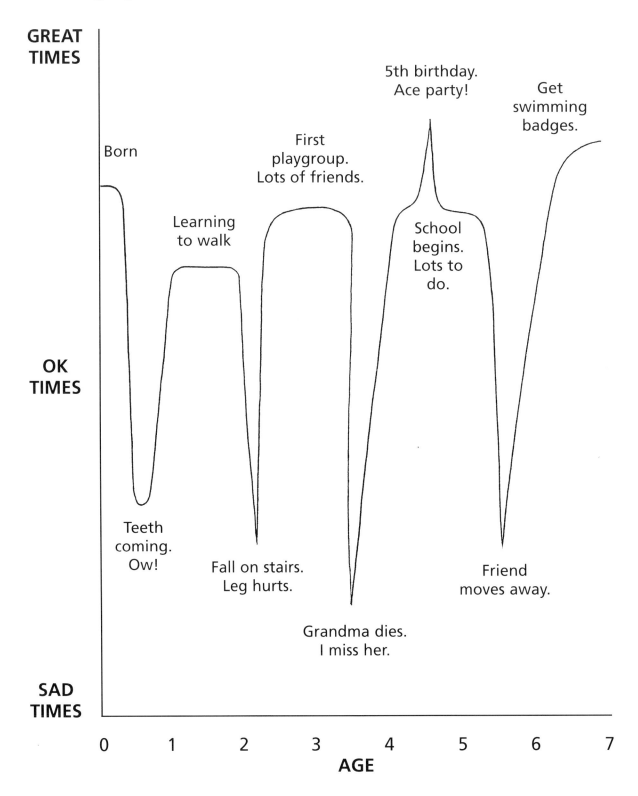

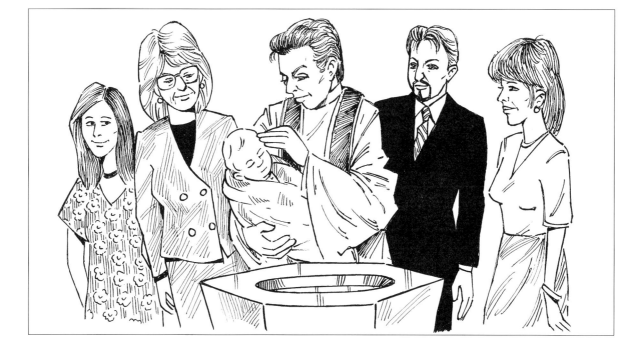

Can you tell what is happening in this picture? It is a special event for many Christians called infant baptism. This usually happens when a baby is a few months old. In the service special words and promises are said. The baby is given a Christian name and the minister says to the baby, 'I baptize you in the name of the Father, Son and Holy Spirit.' He or she also says, 'I sign you with the sign of the cross.' (The cross is a very important symbol in Christianity as it reminds Christians of the death and resurrection of Jesus.)

Many Christians remember the time Jesus was baptized in the River Jordan by John the Baptist. The baptism is also an act of welcome and shows that the baby has been accepted into the church family. (It's not just babies who are baptized. Older children and adults can be baptized as well.)

In Christian infant baptisms the parents make promises in front of God and the church family about bringing up the baby in the Christian faith. They can choose godparents who also promise to trust Jesus and help the baby grow in the Christian faith. Sometimes the baby's family are given a lighted candle to help them remember that the baby belongs to Jesus, the Light of the World.

Time to Think

1. Have you ever made special promises?

2. Is it always easy to keep a promise?

This picture shows a very special way of welcoming babies into a Muslim family. Many Muslim parents want the very first word their baby hears to be 'Allah', the Arabic name for God. The father, grandfather or a family friend will whisper two special prayers which both begin with the words 'Allah is great'.

Into the baby's right ear is whispered the special prayer called the **Adhan** and into the left ear another special prayer called the **Iqamah**. The Adhan is about the call to prayer. The Iqamah tells of the greatness of Allah and invites the newborn baby to belong to him.

In some Muslim countries families like to remember and celebrate two special customs. One custom involves putting something sweet like sugar or honey in the baby's mouth. (This is done very carefully.) The family hopes that the baby will enjoy the taste and also enjoy growing up a Muslim. Another custom followed by some Muslims is cutting the baby's hair shortly after they are born. (Again this is done very carefully.) An amount of money equal to the weight of the hair (or, usually, much more money, as hair is very light) is given to poorer people. Some Muslim parents like to keep the hair as it reminds them of the day their special baby was born.

Muslims sometimes choose their baby's name from the names of the family of Muhammad, the final Prophet. They may ask their leader (called the **Imam**) to choose a name.

Time to Think

1. What special words would you like to say to a newly born baby?

2. Do you know what your name means and why it was chosen?

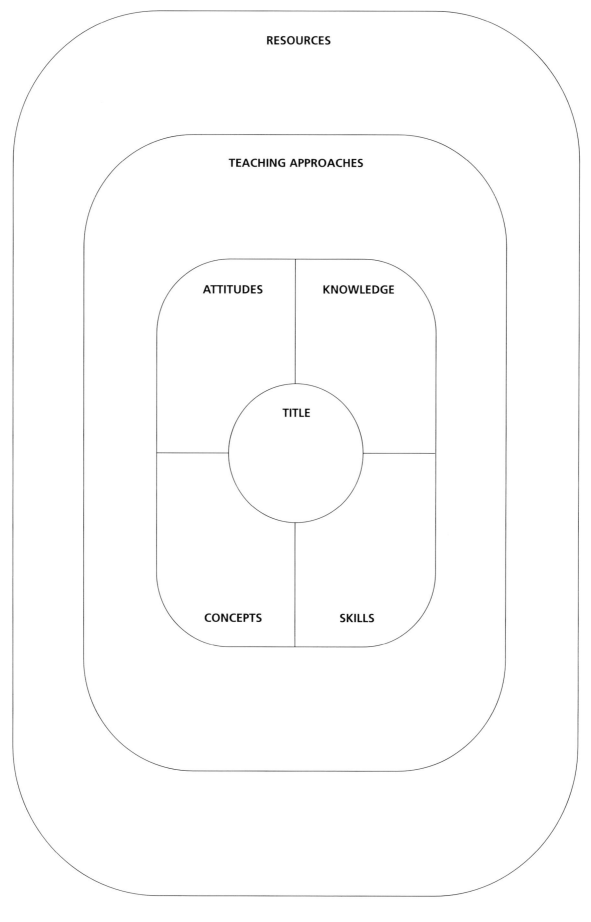

RESOURCES

TEACHING APPROACHES

ATTITUDES   KNOWLEDGE

TITLE

CONCEPTS   SKILLS

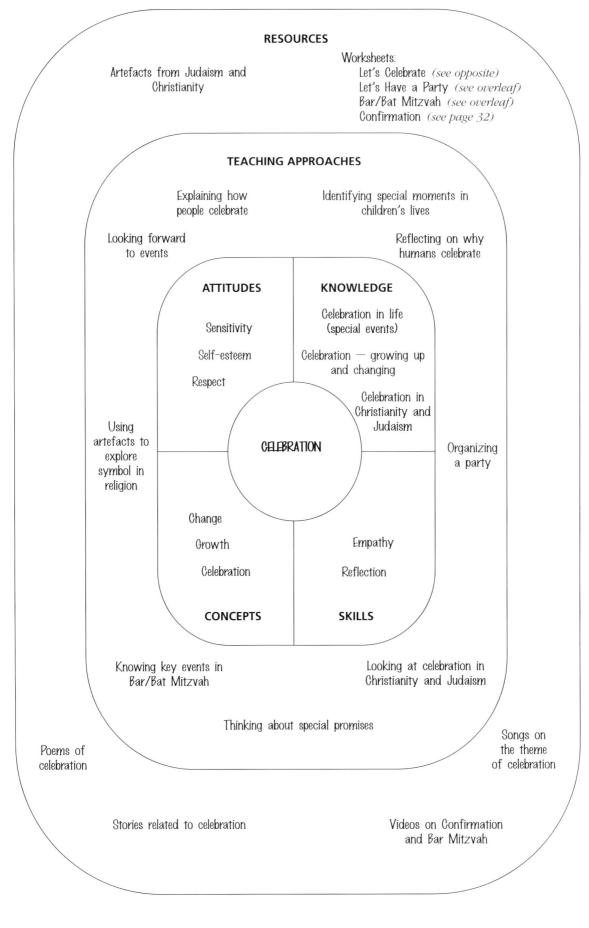

RESOURCES

Artefacts from Judaism and Christianity

Worksheets:
Let's Celebrate *(see opposite)*
Let's Have a Party *(see overleaf)*
Bar/Bat Mitzvah *(see overleaf)*
Confirmation *(see page 32)*

TEACHING APPROACHES

Explaining how people celebrate

Identifying special moments in children's lives

Looking forward to events

Reflecting on why humans celebrate

ATTITUDES

Sensitivity

Self-esteem

Respect

KNOWLEDGE

Celebration in life (special events)

Celebration — growing up and changing

Celebration in Christianity and Judaism

Using artefacts to explore symbol in religion

CELEBRATION

Organizing a party

Change

Growth

Celebration

Empathy

Reflection

CONCEPTS

SKILLS

Knowing key events in Bar/Bat Mitzvah

Looking at celebration in Christianity and Judaism

Thinking about special promises

Poems of celebration

Songs on the theme of celebration

Stories related to celebration

Videos on Confirmation and Bar Mitzvah

Let's Celebrate the Past

Write about or draw a special event which has happened to you.
What made this so special?

Let's Celebrate the Present

Can you think of something that's going to happen soon that you're really looking forward to? Write about or draw it.

Let's Celebrate the Future

Imagine you are ten years older than you are now. What are you looking forward to? Are there some things you're not looking forward to?
Write about or illustrate your answers.

Sam is having a party. There's lots to get ready and he's thinking about all the things he needs to have a really great party. He's already thought of three things. Can you help him fill in the rest?

Friends

What do I need for my party?

Invitations

Presents

Now you've got lots of ideas for planning a party. Which three are the most important ones for you?

1. My most important thing is ....
because ....

2. My second most important thing is ....
because ....

3. My third most important thing is ....
because ....

For many Jewish children one of the most special events in their lives is called, for boys, **Bar Mitzvah** (which means 'son of the Commandment') or, for girls, **Bat Mitzvah** (which means 'daughter of the Commandment'). These special ceremonies take place in a synagogue (the Jewish place of worship). For boys, Bar Mitzvah is celebrated on the first Saturday after their thirteenth birthday. For girls, Bat Mitzvah is after their twelfth birthday. Jews believe that at this age children are old enough to remember and follow the important rules God gave to Moses called the Ten Commandments.

At his Bar Mitzvah the boy must say a prayer and read from part of the **Torah**, the Jewish holy scriptures, which are written in **Hebrew**. For some Jewish children this is like reading a new language, so they have special classes where they can learn more about Hebrew and the Jewish faith. It can be very nerve-racking for the children to read from the Torah at their Bar Mitzvah or Bat Mitzvah. This is because it will be the first time they do this at the synagogue with lots of family and friends there.

It is also when a boy wears a Jewish prayer-shawl, called a **tallit**, for the first time. Only adults wear these so the boy is now a man in the eyes of the Jewish community. After Bar Mitzvah Jewish boys may also wear the special black leather boxes called **tefillin** at times of prayer and worship. Inside the tefillin are words from the Torah.

Time to Think

1. Do you have any important rules you try to follow? What are they?

2. Have you ever read a story, poem or book which helped to guide you in your life? How was it able to help?

There are millions of Christians in the world. Many Christians belong to particular groups or **denominations**. In England two of the largest groups are the **Church of England** and the **Roman Catholic** church. In both denominations there is an important service called **Confirmation.**

Holy Communion is a special meal of bread and wine when Christians remember Jesus and celebrate the belief that he gave his life for them. In the Roman Catholic church children usually begin to take Communion at the age of six or seven and Confirmation is at about twelve years of age. In the Church of England children are usually confirmed between the ages of eleven and sixteen but do not take Communion before this.

Confirmation is a sign that the young person now wishes to be a full member of the church and to take on the responsibilities of the Christian faith for themselves. A special service is held where a bishop, an important leader in these churches, asks God to help the young people grow in the Christian faith and **confirm** the promises made by parents and godparents when the young person was baptized as a baby. In the Church of England the Confirmation usually ends with all those who have been confirmed taking bread and wine in the special Holy Communion service.

Time to Think

1. Have you ever had to prepare for a special event? What did you need to do?

2. Can you think of any food and drink that you only have at special times? What makes it important for you?

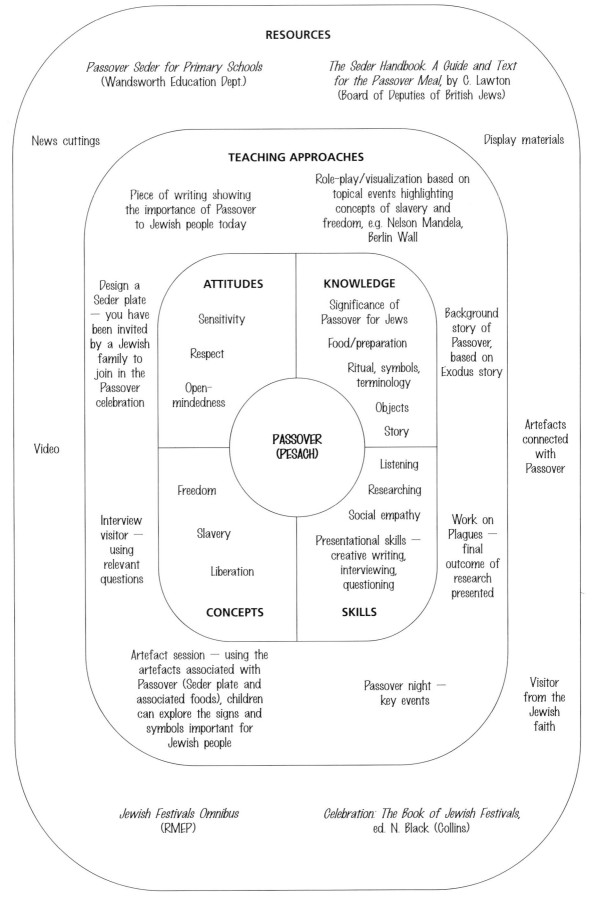

RESOURCES

Passover Seder for Primary Schools
(Wandsworth Education Dept.)

*The Seder Handbook: A Guide and Text
for the Passover Meal,* by C. Lawton
(Board of Deputies of British Jews)

News cuttings

Display materials

TEACHING APPROACHES

Piece of writing showing
the importance of Passover
to Jewish people today

Role-play/visualization based on
topical events highlighting
concepts of slavery and
freedom, e.g. Nelson Mandela,
Berlin Wall

Design a
Seder plate
— you have
been invited
by a Jewish
family to
join in the
Passover
celebration

ATTITUDES

Sensitivity

Respect

Open-
mindedness

KNOWLEDGE

Significance of
Passover for Jews

Food/preparation

Ritual, symbols,
terminology

Objects

Story

Background
story of
Passover,
based on
Exodus story

Video

**PASSOVER
(PESACH)**

Listening

Researching

Social empathy

Presentational skills —
creative writing,
interviewing,
questioning

Artefacts
connected
with
Passover

Interview
visitor —
using
relevant
questions

Freedom

Slavery

Liberation

Work on
Plagues —
final
outcome of
research
presented

CONCEPTS

SKILLS

Artefact session — using the
artefacts associated with
Passover (Seder plate and
associated foods), children
can explore the signs and
symbols important for
Jewish people

Passover night —
key events

Visitor
from the
Jewish
faith

Jewish Festivals Omnibus
(RMEP)

Celebration: The Book of Jewish Festivals,
ed. N. Black (Collins)

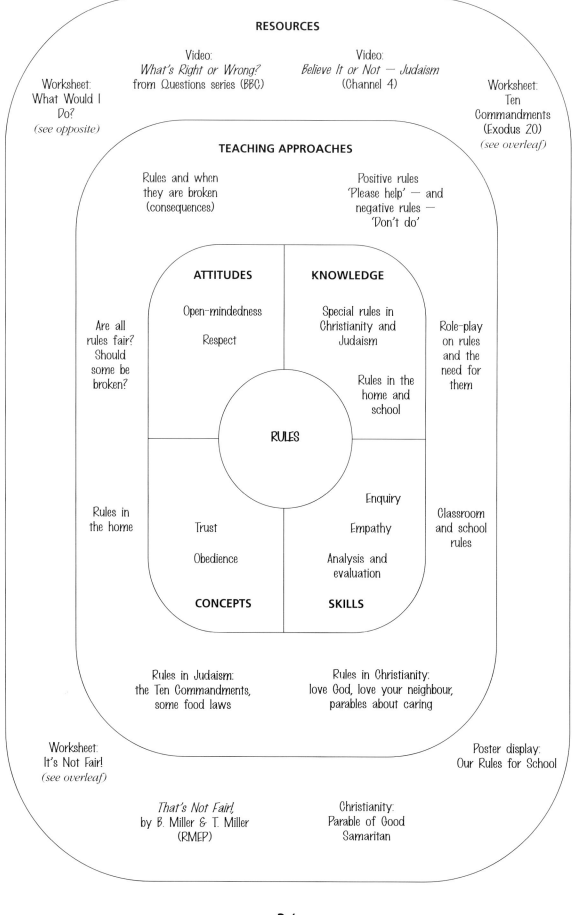

RESOURCES

Video:
What's Right or Wrong?
from Questions series (BBC)

Video:
Believe It or Not — Judaism
(Channel 4)

Worksheet:
What Would I
Do?
(see opposite)

Worksheet:
Ten
Commandments
(Exodus 20)
(see overleaf)

TEACHING APPROACHES

Rules and when
they are broken
(consequences)

Positive rules
'Please help' — and
negative rules —
'Don't do'

Are all
rules fair?
Should
some be
broken?

ATTITUDES

Open-mindedness

Respect

KNOWLEDGE

Special rules in
Christianity and
Judaism

Rules in the
home and
school

Role-play
on rules
and the
need for
them

RULES

Rules in
the home

Trust

Obedience

Enquiry

Empathy

Analysis and
evaluation

Classroom
and school
rules

CONCEPTS

SKILLS

Rules in Judaism:
the Ten Commandments,
some food laws

Rules in Christianity:
love God, love your neighbour,
parables about caring

Worksheet:
It's Not Fair!
(see overleaf)

Poster display:
Our Rules for School

That's Not Fair!
by B. Miller & T. Miller
(RMEP)

Christianity:
Parable of Good
Samaritan

For a long time Joe has really wanted a leather football. He's been saving his pocket money for weeks and he knows exactly the one he wants. It's in the colours of his favourite team and it costs £10. So far he's saved £5 but that seems to have taken ages. He wishes he could have the ball now but he knows he has to save some more money.

One day at school Joe is doing Art (one of his favourite activities) when he realizes that his special drawing pen is in his coat pocket. He asks the teacher if he can pop to the cloakroom and get the pen. 'OK but hurry up, Joe,' replies his teacher.

Joe quickly goes to the cloakroom and grabs his pen. He's just turning to go back when he sees a £5 note lying in the corner of the cloakroom. Five pounds! Just the right amount to get the football! But what about the person who has lost the money? They must be really worried. Joe stops to think for a moment. What is he going to do? What might happen next?

If Joe keeps the money how do you think he will feel?	If Joe hands in the money how do you think he will feel?

'It's not fair!'

How many times have you said these words? It's probably hundreds!
What do you think 'fair' means? Here are some sentences about being fair.
Talk with your friends and teachers about what 'fair' means in each one.

'It's not fair! We never have chips for tea!'

'It's not fair! Sheila always stays up later than me and she's only two years older!'

'It's not fair! Some children in our world will have no presents at all at Christmas time.'

'It's not fair! John always finishes his sums first and gets more right than I do.'

'It's not fair! I'm the only one who ever does any jobs in our house.'

'It's not fair! We should look after animals, not be cruel to them.'

The things in our world that I think are unfair are ...	The world would be more fair if we could ...

For Jewish people the most important rules they follow are called the Ten Commandments. These were given to Moses on Mount Sinai. (You can read more about Moses by looking up Exodus, chapter 20 in the Bible.)

Many Jews, and other people as well, believe keeping the Ten Commandments will help people to lead a good and happy life. Some of the Commandments are about God, some about how human beings should treat one another. Here's what the Ten Commandments say:

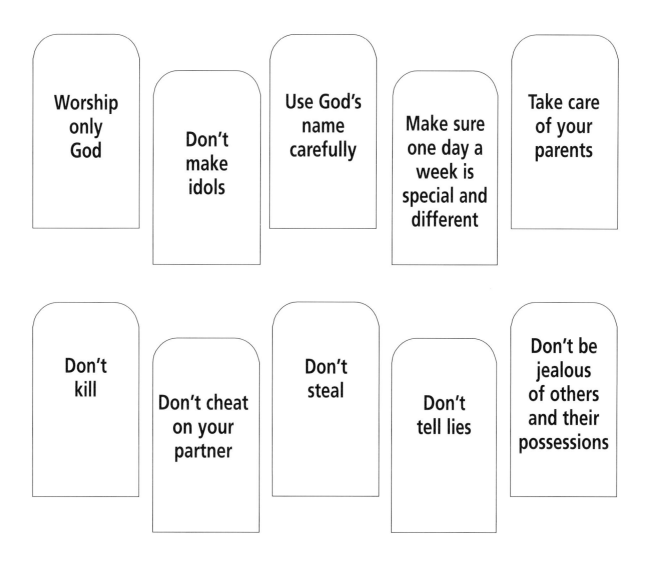

Worship only God

Don't make idols

Use God's name carefully

Make sure one day a week is special and different

Take care of your parents

Don't kill

Don't cheat on your partner

Don't steal

Don't tell lies

Don't be jealous of others and their possessions

Time to Think

1. Which of the Commandments are the hardest to follow?

2. Do you have any important rules for your life?
   What are they?

TOPIC/THEME/MODULE TITLE:

PROGRAMMES OF STUDY	STATEMENTS OF ATTAINMENT	TEACHING/LEARNING EXPERIENCES

AGREED SYLLABUS AREAS OF STUDY:

RESOURCES	METHODS OF ASSESSMENT	CURRICULUM LINKS

SKILLS FOCUS

Reflection	❏
Empathy	❏
Communication	❏
Analysis and evaluation	❏
Reasoning	❏
Enquiry	❏

ATTITUDES FOCUS

Respect	❏
Open-mindedness	❏
Self-esteem	❏
Sensitivity	❏
Critical awareness	❏
Appreciation and wonder	❏

TOPIC/THEME/MODULE TITLE: THE ENVIRONMENT   **AGREED SYLLABUS AREAS OF STUDY:**   AT1 — Questions of meaning, relationships and values
AT2 — Knowledge and understanding of religions

PROGRAMMES OF STUDY	STATEMENTS OF ATTAINMENT	TEACHING/LEARNING EXPERIENCES	RESOURCES	METHODS OF ASSESSMENT	CURRICULUM LINKS
KS 1/2: Key objectives **Helping children to:** * Reflect on the local environment and their place within it * Be aware of important feelings and emotions such as awe and wonder * Explore aspects of human experiences which raise questions about the meaning of life and how religions have responded to them * Experience and respond to the natural world * Study the cycle of nature and the ecological effects of human activity, e.g. soil erosion, destruction of rainforest and ozone layer	**KS1/2: AT1** **Children should be able to:** * Identify examples of our dependence on the earth's resources and be able to demonstrate some expressions of gratitude for the products of the earth * Give examples of how people show that their religion is important to them * Identify some religious stories * Demonstrate an understanding that some questions have religious 'answers' * Show how language and stories can have meaning beyond their literal sense	* Exploring our senses *(see opposite)* * Exploring the classroom environment — noticing new things, finding your way round blindfold * Exploring the school grounds or local environment * Problems in the environment — identifying key issues * Collage work — 'good' and 'bad' things in our world *(see also individual worksheet on page 44)* * How did life begin? Exploring two/three creation stories *(see overleaf)* * Exploring songs, poems and stories about the environment today	*Exploring a Theme — The Environment and Green Beliefs — Valued World* (OEM) *Stations of the Forest* (CAFOD slide pack) *Trees of Life and Hope for the Earth* (Christian Aid poster packs) *Catching the Light and Somewhere to Be,* by B. Moses (WWF) *The Green Umbrella* (WWF) *Creation,* by P. Emmett & S. Hart (Folens primary RE topic pack) *Creation Stories,* by M. Lynch (BFSS National RE Centre) *Worlds of Difference,* by M. Palmer & E. Bisset (WWF) *Hiawatha's Childhood,* by M. Longfellow *Rain Forest* (WWF video material in *Assembly Kit,* BBC)	* Collage work highlighting good and bad aspects of the environment * Recall of key aspects of issues related to the environment	*Science* — knowing that human activity may produce changes in the environment *Art* — communicating ideas and feelings in visual form *English* — developing speaking and listening skills through group discussion *Environmental Education* — recognizing how human lives and livelihoods are dependent upon the environment — recognizing conflicts which arise about environmental issues
				SKILLS FOCUS Reflection ✔ Empathy ✔ Communication ☐ Analysis and evaluation ☐ Reasoning ☐ Enquiry ✔ **ATTITUDES FOCUS** Respect ✔ Open-mindedness ☐ Self-esteem ✔ Sensitivity ☐ Critical awareness ☐ Appreciation and wonder ✔	

The Environment: Some Ideas

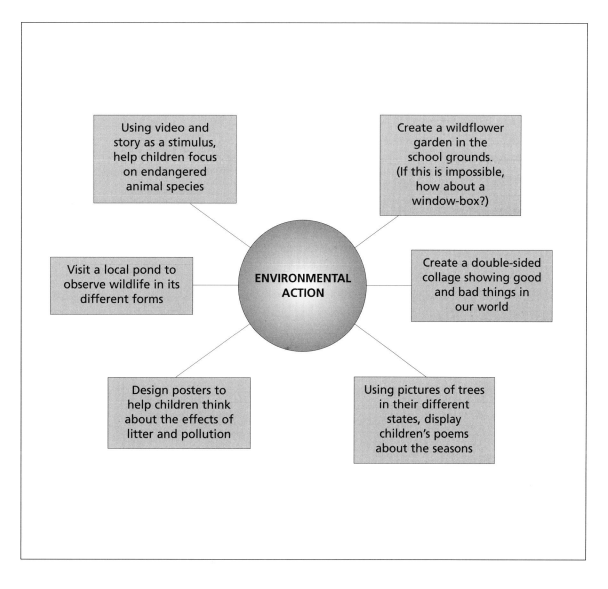

♦ Using Senses

The purpose of this exercise is to help children develop the use of their senses through identifying a variety of substances.

Divide the class into four groups, each of which will be allowed to use only one of the four senses taste, touch, smell and sight.

Place six jamjars containing various substances on a desk. Each group in turn, using only the sense they have been allocated, has to identify the substance within each jar. Each decision must be agreed by the group.

The teacher quickly checks their answers and if any are wrong (there are usually several wrong!) the group then uses another sense to try and identify the substance. The idea is that all groups will need to use several senses before they can identify all the substances.

In the beginning God created the heavens and the earth. Before this there was only God. Nothing else at all. On the first day God said, 'Let there be light.' There was light and the light was separate from the dark. The light was called day and the darkness night. 'It's a good start,' thought God, 'but there's still a lot left to do.'

On the second day God separated the water from the sky. 'It's better,' said God, 'but there's still a lot to do.'

On the third day God separated the dry ground (called land) from the sea. 'This is good,' said God, 'but there's still more to do.' God created all kinds of plants and seeds that would produce fruit. This had been a very busy day. 'It looks even better now,' said God, 'but there's still a long way to go.'

On the fourth day God created the sun (the greater light which covered the day) and the moon (the light that governed the night) and he also made the stars. 'This is looking beautiful already,' said God, 'but there's still more to do.'

On the fifth day God created all kinds of creatures to live in the sea and all kinds of birds to decorate the sky. This had been another very busy day. 'The world is getting busier,' thought God, 'but I haven't finished yet.'

On the sixth day God created the creatures of the land. There were wild animals and tame animals, all different shapes and sizes. God liked what he had created so far but he still hadn't finished. 'I will make a man, in the image of me,' he said. 'I will put man in charge of my world but he must look after it carefully.' So God created man. 'This is very special,' thought God.

On the seventh day God had finished his work so he rested. 'One day should be special and holy and different to all the rest,' said God.

Soon God noticed that the man he had created was lonely and needed a friend. While the man (whose name was Adam) was sleeping God took one of his ribs and created a woman (her name was Eve). Now everything seemed perfect. Adam and Eve lived in a beautiful garden with everything they needed. It looked as if this beauty and happiness would last for ever ... but it didn't.

Time to Think

1. What happens next in this story?

2. Is it good to have one day which is 'different'? Why?

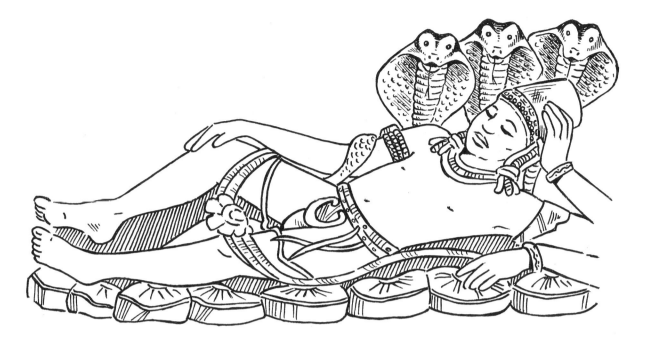

Before the world there was nothing but ocean. In the ocean lay Lord Vishnu, the Preserver, who was resting by a giant water snake. Vishnu looked across the huge calm waters. He now felt it was the right time to start the world. Before his eyes appeared Lord Brahma, the Creator god, sitting in a lotus blossom, ready to obey Vishnu.

Brahma divided the lotus flower into three parts which became known as earth, sky and heaven. Next he placed all kinds of plants, animals and insects. The world was already a marvellous place but Brahma knew his work was not yet complete. The world still needed someone to care for it. So Brahma split himself in two to create male and female. The female was called Shatarupa, which means 'mysterious', and the male was a man called Manu, which means 'wise'. Shatarupa and Manu walked together into the beautiful world, the first people to obey Lord Vishnu and care for the world.

Everything in the world comes from Brahma, who is part of the Supreme One. At the end of this universe, the world and Brahma, like all before and all to come, will be destroyed by Lord Shiva, the Destroyer.

Time to Think

1. Is it easier to create or destroy? Why?

2. Can you think of someone who is wise? What gives them this important quality?

What a Wonderful World!
What makes our world sometimes seem so beautiful? Draw or write about your favourite things in our world.

What an Ugly World!
Sometimes our world can seem a real mess. Draw or write about things which spoil our world.

TOPIC/THEME/MODULE TITLE: EASTER AGREED SYLLABUS AREAS OF STUDY: Religious belief, practice and expression

PROGRAMMES OF STUDY	STATEMENTS OF ATTAINMENT	TEACHING/LEARNING EXPERIENCES	RESOURCES	METHODS OF ASSESSMENT	CURRICULUM LINKS
Key Stage 1: Key objectives **Helping children to:** * Be aware of important feelings and emotions such as love and forgiveness * Explore those aspects of human experiences which raise questions about the meaning of life * Be introduced to key religious founders, e.g. Jesus * Hear about some religious festivals — their stories and celebrations * Explore how people's beliefs can be expressed in different ways	**Children should be able to:** * Identify ways people, including religious believers, show care for others * Explain that some people act in particular ways because of their religious beliefs * Give examples of how people show that their religion is important to them	* Focus on 'Someone I'd like to meet' * Exploring feelings associated with Easter through story (e.g. *Dogger*, by S. Hughes, linking 'lost and found', sadness and joy) * Special customs at Easter, e.g. hot cross buns, eggs (linked to theme of new life) * Exploring worship at Easter (use of palms and candles) * Creating an Easter display, e.g. greetings-cards, Easter garden (as way of telling story) * Highlighting key aspects of Easter story (entry into Jerusalem, Last Supper, Crucifixion, Resurrection) * Visitors to share why Easter is special for them * Listening to and talking about songs related to Easter * Christian artefacts related to Easter (*See also chart overleaf.*)	*Teaching RE: Easter 5–14* (OEM) *Easter, Holy Week, Shrove Tuesday, Ash Wednesday and Mardi Gras; Christian Festivals. Teacher's Book* (Living Festivals Series, RMEP) *The Lion Easter Book*, by M. Batchelor (Lion) *Easter*, by J. Pienkowski (Puffin) *Easter: A Story and Activity Book*, by R. James (Macdonald) *Easter*, by O. Gibbons (Hodder & Stoughton) *Feasting for Festivals*, by J. Wilson (Lion) *High Days and Holidays*, by D. Self (Lion)	**Assessing children's understanding by their ability to:** * Recall key events in the Easter story * Recognize and explain some symbols associated with Easter	*D & T* – designing and developing Easter cards *English* – articulating ideas about feelings and emotions *Music* – listening to a range of music (classical, jazz, rock, pop) related to Easter

SKILLS FOCUS

Reflection	☑
Empathy	☐
Communication	☑
Analysis and evaluation	☐
Reasoning	☐
Enquiry	☐

ATTITUDES FOCUS

Respect	☑
Open-mindedness	☐
Self-esteem	☑
Sensitivity	☐
Critical awareness	☐
Appreciation and wonder	☑

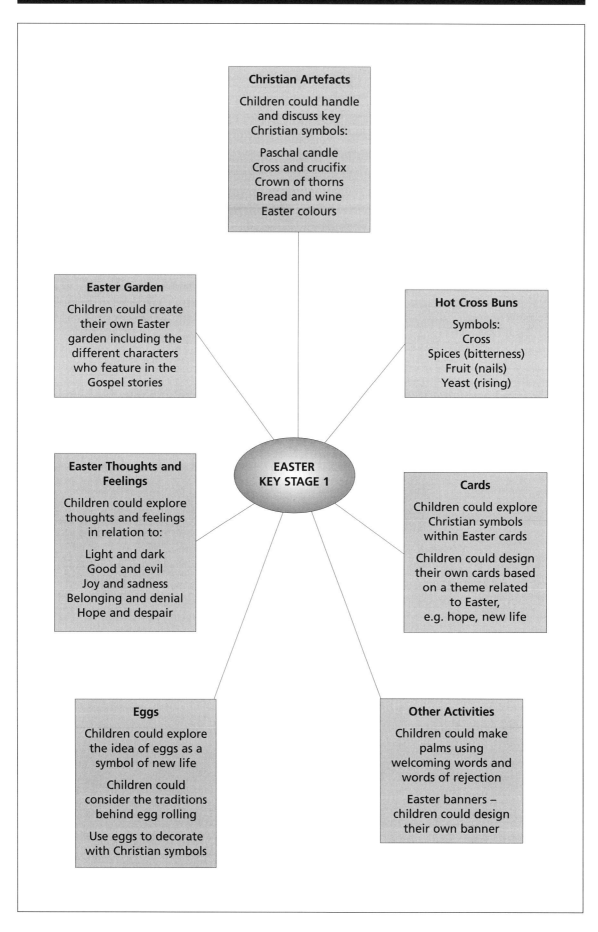

Christian Artefacts

Children could handle and discuss key Christian symbols:

Paschal candle
Cross and crucifix
Crown of thorns
Bread and wine
Easter colours

Easter Garden

Children could create their own Easter garden including the different characters who feature in the Gospel stories

Hot Cross Buns

Symbols:
Cross
Spices (bitterness)
Fruit (nails)
Yeast (rising)

Easter Thoughts and Feelings

Children could explore thoughts and feelings in relation to:

Light and dark
Good and evil
Joy and sadness
Belonging and denial
Hope and despair

EASTER KEY STAGE 1

Cards

Children could explore Christian symbols within Easter cards

Children could design their own cards based on a theme related to Easter, e.g. hope, new life

Eggs

Children could explore the idea of eggs as a symbol of new life

Children could consider the traditions behind egg rolling

Use eggs to decorate with Christian symbols

Other Activities

Children could make palms using welcoming words and words of rejection

Easter banners – children could design their own banner

TOPIC/THEME/MODULE TITLE: EASTER

AGREED SYLLABUS AREAS OF STUDY: Religious belief, practice and expression

PROGRAMMES OF STUDY	STATEMENTS OF ATTAINMENT	TEACHING/LEARNING EXPERIENCES	RESOURCES	METHODS OF ASSESSMENT	CURRICULUM LINKS
Key Stage 2: Key objectives **Helping children to:** * Understand important feelings and emotions * Explore those aspects of human experiences which raise questions about the meaning of life * Develop an understanding of other people's points of view and experiences * Become familiar with key passages in the Bible and their influence on religious belief * Study a major Christian festival	**Children should be able to:** * Show how language and story can have meaning beyond their literal sense * Make connections between observable features of Christianity * Recognize and name some important symbols * Give examples of ways in which religious belief has made a profound difference to someone's life	* Exploring the Easter story through the eyes of the characters involved (the Jewish leaders, the disciples, the Roman soldiers) * Looking closely at the story and sequencing key events *(see overleaf)* * Exploring the Resurrection in terms of contrasts (sadness and joy, leaving and returning, despair and hope, death and new life) * Using visitors as a way of exploring Christian belief today * Exploring key themes in the Easter story (love, sacrifice, trust) through drama and songs * Linking the Easter story to Judaism (developed through work on Passover)	*Teaching RE: Easter 5–14* (OEM) *Easter, Holy Week: Shrove Tuesday, Ash Wednesday and Mardi Gras; Christian Festivals. Teacher's Book* (Living Festivals Series, RMEP) *The Lion Easter Book,* by M. Batchelor (Lion) *Easter,* by J. Pienkowski (Puffin) *Easter: A Story and Activity Book,* by R. James (Macdonald) *Easter,* by O. Gibbons (Hodder & Stoughton) *Feasting for Festivals,* by J. Wilson (Lion) *High Days and Holidays,* by D. Self (Lion)	**Children could:** * Produce a diary of the last week of Jesus' life showing events in their sequential order * Show some evidence of thinking about the issues related to the 'truth' of the Resurrection **SKILLS FOCUS** Reflection ☐ Empathy ☐ Communication ☑ Analysis and evaluation ☑ Reasoning ☐ Enquiry ☐ **ATTITUDES FOCUS** Respect ☑ Open-mindedness ☑ Self-esteem ☐ Sensitivity ☐ Critical awareness ☑ Appreciation and wonder ☐	*English* — speaking and listening, articulating ideas *Drama* — exploring themes through role-play *Music* — appreciating different kinds of music associated with the Easter story

Jane and Phil are working on the Easter story but they keep getting the events mixed up in the wrong order. Can you help them follow the journey? Number the statements below in the right order.

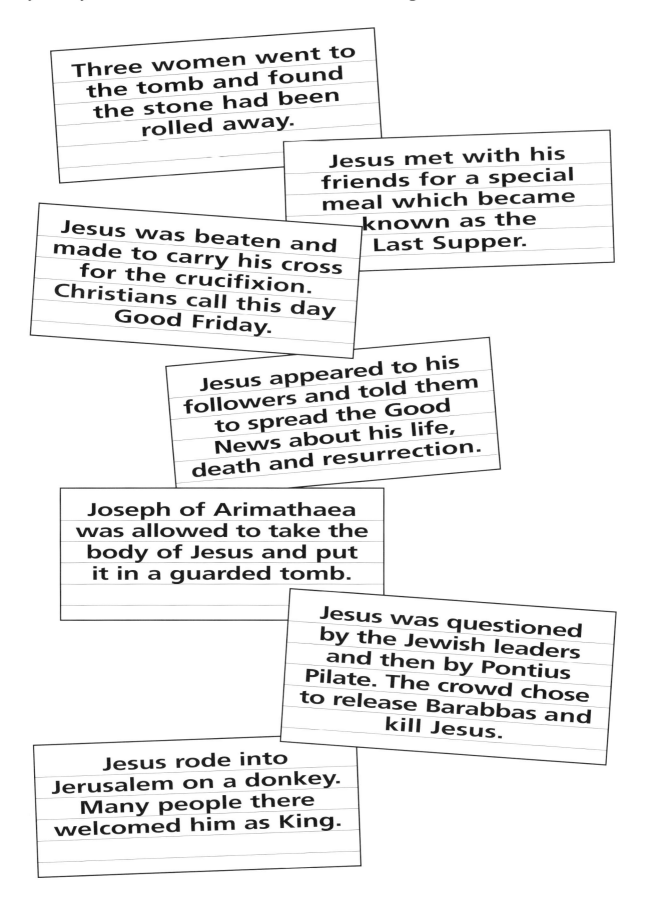

Three women went to the tomb and found the stone had been rolled away.

Jesus met with his friends for a special meal which became known as the Last Supper.

Jesus was beaten and made to carry his cross for the crucifixion. Christians call this day Good Friday.

Jesus appeared to his followers and told them to spread the Good News about his life, death and resurrection.

Joseph of Arimathaea was allowed to take the body of Jesus and put it in a guarded tomb.

Jesus was questioned by the Jewish leaders and then by Pontius Pilate. The crowd chose to release Barabbas and kill Jesus.

Jesus rode into Jerusalem on a donkey. Many people there welcomed him as King.

Co-ordinating RE in Your School

So far in this chapter we have thought about the importance of developing effective policy statements and planning schemes of work in RE. For the remainder of the chapter we shall look at the management and co-ordination of RE and how RE can be approached in the classroom through a variety of themes and schemes.

It goes without saying that the RE Co-ordinator has a critical role in enhancing children's' learning experiences in RE. The RE role can often seem a thankless task and the RE Co-ordinator does have in some ways a more challenging and sensitive role than other co-ordinators. I've yet to hear, for example, of teachers who wish to withdraw from teaching Maths on the grounds of their conscience (although there may be all kinds of other reasons why they would like to avoid teaching Maths!). Religion for many teachers is a controversial and emotive area and is likely to be viewed with greater concern than some other subject areas. It follows therefore that the RE Co-ordinator's role doesn't just need a specific knowledge base but requires sensitivity and wisdom in helping colleagues recognize that RE does make a valuable contribution to children's learning. The charts below and overleaf highlight some of the key functions in becoming an effective RE Co-ordinator.

KEY PRINCIPLES IN THE ROLE OF THE RE CO-ORDINATOR

Good co-ordination of RE involves:

- Being willing to listen to and think through the genuine concerns many teachers have about delivering RE effectively.

- Trying new ideas in teaching RE and being prepared to discuss successes and failures.

- Encouraging the Governors and Headteacher to invest time and support for developing good RE.

- Planning work which has rigour, breadth and balance and stimulates children's interest.

- Ensuring resources are helpful, contemporary and stimulating.

- Involving the school and local community in sharing important events and celebrations which have connections with religion, including well-planned and well-resourced visits and visitors.

- Being realistic about the depth of knowledge and interest colleagues can have in teaching RE.

- Ensuring that your contribution to RE is valued and respected – avoid the feeling that you're ploughing a lone furrow with no support.

- Ensuring that you have positive links with other local schools and the L.E.A. which enhance your own professional development.

THE MANAGEMENT OF RE IN YOUR SCHOOL

Effectively managing RE involves:

- Being familiar with legal requirements for RE, particularly in relation to the requirements of the local Agreed Syllabus (or other relevant document).

- Keeping in touch with local and national developments in RE through participating in courses, reading relevant publications, affiliating to professional RE organizations such as CEM (Christian Education Movement) or PCfRE (Professional Council for RE).

- Creating and developing an RE policy statement which is educationally clear and enthuses the reader about the contributions of RE to children's learning.

- Supporting the school in the development of lively and imaginative schemes of work which provide clear detail, highlight key skills and attitudes, demonstrate links with the Agreed Syllabus, show variety in learning strategies and are effectively assessed and resourced.

- Monitoring and reviewing the delivery of schemes of work in RE through regular meetings with colleagues, sharing classroom work with other teachers, reviewing schemes of work once they have been delivered. N.B. There is some evidence to suggest that a major issue emerging from Ofsted inspections in Key Stage 1 and Key Stage 2 is the effective deployment of school co-ordinators, particularly in relation to the delivery and review of schemes of work. (See pages 59–60.)

- Supporting teachers in the actual delivery of RE through activities such as introducing a new RE topic, sharing ideas about using stories and artefacts in the classroom, suggesting ideas for reflective activities in RE. (See Chapter 5.)

- Leading staff discussions on RE, sharing in the leadership of school-based Inset and fully participating in RE discussions with school pyramids and clusters.

- Obtaining, organizing and managing a good range of RE resources. This includes ensuring that the Headteacher and Governors are aware of funding needs, using inspection copies for colleagues to view, creating and maintaining a list of all available resources, using local teacher's centres and faith communities where feasible.

- Supporting colleagues in the assessment, recording and reporting of RE, with clear guidelines and objectives and reviewing children's progress. (See Chapter 4.)

- Ensuring that progression and continuity are built into schemes of work so that recurring themes and topics are given new insights and material.

- Producing a development plan, agreed with the Headteacher, which is practical and realistic and moves RE forward.

- Ensuring that display work in RE is prominent around the school (especially at parents' evenings!) and that 'special' RE events are publicized in the media.

- Establishing and maintaining positive relationships with the local religious communities, ensuring that there are practical opportunities for children to visit places of worship and talk with members of different religious traditions.

♦ Thinking Through Themes and Schemes

Several times in this book we have mentioned the *implicit* and *explicit* dimensions of RE. It is worth thinking through what we mean by implicit and explicit RE. Implicit RE is primarily concerned with the contribution RE makes to children's spiritual, moral and cultural development. It is the part of RE concerned with the 'inner self', with helping children explore the question 'What does it mean to be me?' This can include helping children reflect on their emotions, their feelings, their relationships with others and the natural world. It is also the part of RE which raises important questions about the purpose and nature of humanity. Themes in which the implicit dimension can provide a main focus include the following:

- Myself
- Communities
- The Environment
- Feelings
- Caring and Sharing
- Light and Dark
- Families

Explicit RE is concerned with introducing children to various aspects of specific religions. In an explicit theme RE is the major contributor to the planning and focus of the topic. Explicit themes include the following:

- Places of Worship
- Pilgrimage
- Religious Festivals
- Sacred Writings
- Key Figures in Religion
- Religious Signs and Symbols
- Worship

It is important for RE co-ordinators to think carefully about the organization of RE within a topic-based approach. As well as making RE an explicit theme there are three other possible means of delivering RE in a thematic context:

- Via a fully integrated topic where RE is one of a number of contributing disciplines, e.g. 'Homes', 'Journeys', 'Stories', 'Celebrations', 'Food', 'Water', 'Rules'.
- Via a topic in which another area is the leading contributor and RE has a supportive role, e.g. 'Colour and Pattern', 'Gifts and Giving', 'Communication', 'The Victorians', 'Life in Britain since 1930'.
- Via a topic in which RE has, at best, tenuous connections and really would benefit from a different focus, e.g. 'Transport', 'Electricity', 'Structures'.

It is important for RE both to fit comfortably in school- or year-based topics but also to retain its own distinct identity as a curriculum subject. Care needs to be taken to ensure that imaginative and lively RE is not hampered by unhelpful or irrelevant themes. This could mean broadening certain themes, e.g. changing 'Transport' into 'Journeys'.

Finally, it is essential to involve the Headteacher and Governors in the development of RE at your school. Ensuring RE has its place on the school development plan, informing Governors of new initiatives and developments in RE and keeping RE in colleagues' minds are all helpful ways of maintaining the status RE deserves.

CHAPTER THREE

An Inspector Calls

Quality Issues in RE

Some Year 1 pupils have been discussing key incidents in the life of Moses. The following gives an indication of both children's uniqueness and the folly of trusting too much in what they may say.

INSPECTOR   This is very interesting work you're doing on Moses. If I wanted to find out more about Moses where would I look?

CHILD 1   On a computer!

CHILD 2   Ask our teacher, she knows lots about Moses.

CHILD 3   You could look it up in the Bible. It's in the part which Christians call the Old Testament, the Book of Exodus. If you want to know about Jesus you have to look in the New Testament. *(The Inspector is suitably impressed by this display of factual recall.)*

CHILD 4   Yes, we've done lots about Jesus in our class.

INSPECTOR   What can you tell me about his life?

CHILD 1   Well, first of all he lived with God in heaven and then he decided it was time to come to earth so he floated down on a cloud, jumped off and landed in a stable.

INSPECTOR   *(recovering poise)* Where was this stable?

CHILD 2   I think it was in Darlington! We remembered Jesus' birthday in our school not very long ago. It has a special name ... It's called D-Day!

CHILD 3   My grandma says Jesus was born in a warm cosy house in Ibiza!

INSPECTOR   What happened to Jesus when he grew up?

CHILD 4   Well, I think he was meant to do God's work but I think he got bored with this after a while so he got a proper job!

The above exchange illustrates the variety of 'understanding' that children bring to RE! The infamous Sod's Law implies that inspectors will inevitably speak to the children you least want them to, and while it may be enormously tempting to 'overhear' these conversations, the preceding dialogue suggests that this may not be such a good idea! This chapter focuses on quality in RE partly through the issues related to inspection but also through the broader issues of quality learning in RE.

The phrase 'we're being inspected' is not one guaranteed to relax busy teachers' state of mind. While inspection is demanding it doesn't have to be seen as life threatening! The criteria for inspection are available in an open public document and, if applied effectively, can lead to higher-quality RE planning, provision and practice.

In essence the inspection of RE is concerned with two key issues:

- Pupil attainment and progress in RE.
- Quality of teaching.

Other important aspects of inspection in RE which also need to be considered are:

- Arrangements for assessment, recording and reporting. (Suggestions for assessment in RE can be found in Chapter 4.)
- The content of the RE programme and its planning (i.e. is RE planned thematically or a discrete subject provision?).
- Provision for pupils with SEN.
- The resourcing and management of the RE curriculum.

◆ RE – Still the Cinderella Subject?

The current picture nationally in RE in Key Stages 1 and 2 is far from encouraging. The tables below and overleaf indicate current strengths and weaknesses and are based on information from Ofsted reports.

Time to Think

1. What are the main priorities for RE in your school?
2. How could you go about meeting these priorities?

STANDARDS OF ACHIEVEMENT/QUALITY OF LEARNING
Many primary schools do not meet the statutory requirements for RE, particularly in KS 1. Standards overall however are sound in 80% of lessons in KS 1. In KS 2 standards are unsatisfactory or poor in almost 30% of lessons.
Good standards are achieved when pupils are given the opportunity to talk about their feelings, develop their understanding of concepts and symbols, and demonstrate both knowledge and understanding of Christianity as a living world-wide faith and awareness of the main features of the other principal religions. Pupils show sensitivity and respect for others who hold beliefs different to their own.
Poor standards occur when provision is patchy with little developed work on what it means to belong to a religion. The RE curriculum is too restrictive, giving pupils little understanding of religious ideas and symbolism. Pupils are not provided with challenging work or asked to question/reflect upon their learning.

QUALITY OF TEACHING

In RE, teaching at KS 1 is of a higher standard than the average for National Curriculum subjects but in KS 2 the standard is lower than the national average.

Good teaching in RE occurs when lessons are well planned with clear objectives, teachers have confidence in their delivery, using correct and appropriate terminology, and develop children's interest in RE through a wide range of resources.

Poor teaching occurs where there is dull exposition of religious belief and practice with a narrow concentration on factual material and a failure to engage pupils in their own interests and concerns. Planning is poor and pupils experience an *ad hoc* approach to delivery which lacks relevance, progression and continuity.

OTHER KEY ISSUES

Assessment, Recording and Reporting
The significant majority of schools in KS 1 and KS 2 have no policy for assessment, recording and reporting in RE. In the few that do, the policy is not related to explicit criteria but is subjective in nature and focuses on children's personal development rather than their progress in RE.

Curriculum Content
Although Agreed Syllabuses have played an important role in enhancing the quality of RE in schools, for many primary schools RE is only loosely related to an Agreed Syllabus. There is a lack of detailed schemes of work, with too many tenuous links between RE and topic work.

SEN Provision
There is little evidence of differentiated work in RE and some pupils are inappropriately withdrawn from both RE and Collective Worship to be given extra help with reading.

Co-ordination, Management and Resources
Some schools do not have co-ordinators' guidelines or any kind of monitoring in RE. There are no specialist RE teachers in the majority of primary schools and there is a major need for Inset support in RE. Schools are often poorly resourced with a barely adequate choice of books and other important resource material.

KEY AREAS FOR IMPROVEMENT

RE can be enhanced in schools through the following:

- Ensuring sufficient time and resources are provided for RE.
- Equipping RE Co-ordinators to support effective planning, delivery and review of the RE curriculum.
- Effectively balancing the teaching of Christianity and the other principal religions, ensuring schemes of work feature progression and continuity.
- Effective RE Inset which gives teachers knowledge and confidence in RE.
- Relating RE to the needs and interests of pupils, encouraging them to question, reflect and evaluate.

Being Successful in RE: Four Key Factors

1. Be Prepared

The criteria for standards of achievement, quality of learning and quality of teaching are not a secret which teachers have to guess: they're clearly published in the Ofsted Framework. Before an inspector has even visited a school they will have formed an impression of the school's provision and practice in RE through the pre-inspection evidence. In an ideal world it would be extremely helpful to have the following documentation available:

- *Agreed Syllabus* or other appropriate document.
- *RE policy statement* which has the agreement and support of staff and governors.
- *Schemes of work for each year group* (see Chapter 2 for differing approaches to schemes of work). It is helpful to provide evidence of how RE is to be organized, e.g. RE may be delivered through identified themes or as a discrete subject. It is also useful to indicate how recurring themes (e.g. celebrations within Christianity like Christmas, Easter and Harvest) build progression into children's learning.
- *Staffing of RE*, including any specialist co-ordination and delivery.
- *Inset in RE*, both school based and opportunities for professional development outside the school context.
- *Spending on RE and resource provision.*
- *RE's contribution to the broader curriculum*, especially in terms of children's spiritual, moral, social and cultural development.
- *Links with the local community*, especially in terms of the local faith community(ies).
- *Development plan for RE* which clearly states priorities for future development.
- *Withdrawals from RE*, i.e. the number of children actually withdrawn from RE.
- *Any policies* (either RE or whole-school focused) *on assessment, recording, reporting, differentiation and provision for SEN children.*

Time to Think

How is my school doing in relation to the documentation outlined above?

FRAMEWORK FOR A GOOD RE CURRICULUM

A good curriculum which promotes learning involves children:

- Using a range of ideas to describe important beliefs and practices (e.g. pictures, models, role-play and drama, stories).

- Having access to a wide range of resources, e.g. artefacts, food, stories, visits and visitors, pictures and photographs, music and video.

- Experiencing a wide range of activities which focus on attainment in RE.

- Being encouraged to learn and use specialist language in RE (e.g. 'mosque', 'gurdwara', 'synagogue').

- Developing their knowledge and understanding of Christianity as a living world-wide faith (e.g. being able to talk about key Christian beliefs and practices).

- Developing their knowledge and understanding of the other principal religions in Great Britain (not all at once though!), e.g. children learning about Islam could talk about the Five Pillars and their importance for Muslims.

- Understanding that there are questions in life which are puzzling – e.g. 'How did life begin?' or 'What happens when someone dies?' – and that religions have responded to these questions with different beliefs.

- Recognizing that for some people religion is the most special and important part of their lives and it affects their whole lifestyle.

- Successfully 'living out' in practice the skills and attitudes developed in RE, e.g. handling and using religious artefacts with care and sensitivity or showing an understanding of why some practices which at first sight appear strange and unfamiliar are actually a central part of a person's faith.

- Being encouraged to ask open-ended questions and to relate their learning in RE to their own thoughts, feelings and experiences.

- Developing skills of collaboration and reflection in the classroom.

2. Consider Carefully the Children's Achievement and Learning in RE

An essential question for any RE teacher to consider is: 'What difference does this series of lessons in RE make to children and their learning?' It is particularly important to think about the gains made by children in the knowledge, understanding, skills and attitudes which form the framework of RE in your school. The table opposite suggests a framework for promoting good standards of achievement and quality of learning in RE. The table below looks at situations in which RE is struggling.

Time to Think

1. What do you consider to be the most important factors in enabling children to learn effectively?
2. What immediate steps do you need to take to improve the quality of learning in RE in your school?

A POOR RE CURRICULUM OCCURS WHEN
• There are few resources accessible to children.
• Questions of an open-ended nature raised by children are either ignored or dealt with in a token manner.
• The range of learning activities is severely limited, e.g. listen to the story, draw the picture.
• Children are not encouraged to look beyond the external features of a religion and consider what it means to belong to a religion.
• Skills and attitudes are not actively encouraged to grow.
• Little attention is given to correct use of specialist religious terms.
• Little or no attempt is made to assess children's achievements and learning in RE.
• There is little or no evidence of children recalling previous learning, working collaboratively with others, or reflecting upon their learning and making clear gains in their knowledge and understanding.

3. Think Carefully about the Quality of Teaching in RE

No-one (except the most 'ignorant' of people) has ever suggested that teaching RE is a doddle. The very nature of the subject means it requires considerable skill, understanding and sensitivity. RE clearly has its own field of enquiry but is also concerned with children's spiritual, moral, social and cultural development. As a lead player in the 'conscience' of the curriculum, RE is directly interested in children's emotions, feelings, thoughts and experiences. This approach to RE, recognizing that religion remains a controversial area for many people, can create some tensions and concerns for the teacher, but RE teaching should be characterized by the effective deployment of a range of teaching strategies. Sometimes teachers can limit their teaching strategies in RE but effective learning takes place when children are able to experience different learning activities. The following methods could collectively create a rich diet for children to engage in:

- Stillness and reflection • Discussion • Role-play • Dance • Drama and movement • Art • Music • Listening to visitors • Opportunity to question visitors • Writing (poems, stories, diaries) • Exploring artefacts
- Visiting places of worship • Story • Modelling • Using IT
- Using video • D & T (especially in relation to foods and artefacts)

The table at the top of the page opposite sets out some suggestions for enhancing the quality of teaching in RE. It is important to remember, though, that an Ofsted inspection is not the best time to suddenly change your teaching strategies. If you are not comfortable with drama, the sudden introduction of it into a lesson will only create confusion in children's minds. It is also a feature of some RE lessons that they begin really well with clear objectives but then 'fizzle out' with no opportunity to summarize the gains made in the learning. It is really helpful to spend a few minutes at the end of a lesson pulling together the different strands of learning that have been developed.

Time to Think

1. What are your preferred methods of teaching in relation to RE?
2. Which strategies would you like to develop? How could you go about this?

4. Consider Doing Your Own Review of RE in Your School

There is some evidence emerging from Ofsted inspections in Key Stages 1 and 2 that a vital issue facing schools is the effective deployment of subject co-ordinators. Co-ordinators are often involved in the planning stage but sometimes have no opportunity either to teach in classes other than their own or to monitor and review the progress of their subject in their school. The role of the RE Co-ordinator has been dealt with more fully in the previous chapter but it is worth considering here how the RE Co-ordinator can review progress in their school.

The lower table opposite sets out the practical issues involved in reviewing RE and the table overleaf lists the key questions a school needs to address.

GOOD TEACHING IN RE INVOLVES

- Having clear and appropriate objectives which are shared in such way as to enable children to know what they are doing and why they are doing it.

- Well-paced lessons which use different contexts (whole-class, group, paired and individual work) to promote learning.

- Deploying a range of strategies and activities and not limiting RE to a narrow diet of story and colouring in pictures.

- Using a range of appropriate and contemporary resources.

- Continually supporting and monitoring individual children's progress.

- Providing regular feedback to children which enables them to make further gains in their learning.

- Creating a classroom ethos where children feel safe and secure and therefore able to share important aspects of their own lives without the fear of embarrassment or ridicule.

- Celebrating children's successes and achievements.

- Effectively balancing the 'implicit' aspects of RE with the 'explicit' aspects.

- Creating a learning environment which supports children's learning in RE through effective display work (posters, pictures, children's work, artefacts, relevant books).

EFFECTIVE REVIEW OF RE INVOLVES

- Having clear aims and objectives for RE.

- Encouraging a broad range of teaching and learning styles.

- Continually highlighting the key skills and attitudes RE is concerned with.

- Ensuring provision for SEN pupils is both planned and delivered.

- Demonstrating that RE schemes of work and actual practice provide for differentiated learning and considering carefully issues of progression and continuity.

- Providing and reviewing guidance on assessment, recording and reporting in RE.

- Creating and reviewing a yearly development plan which is practical and realistic.

- Reviewing and updating resource provision.

KEY QUESTIONS FOR REVIEW

- How have children developed in their spiritual, moral, social and cultural awareness through their learning in RE?

- What range of learning experiences and resources do children encounter in RE?

- How have the requirements of the Agreed Syllabus been incorporated into the school's RE programme?

- What gains have children made in their knowledge and understanding of Christianity as a living world-wide faith?

- What gains have children made in their knowledge and understanding of the other principal religions which the school covers?

- How is the children's progress in RE assessed, recorded and reported?

- How has the local community been involved in the delivery of RE?

- Have children had the opportunity to experience RE which has been carefully planned and delivered with both knowledge and interest?

CHAPTER FOUR

Assessment in RE

The local Minister genuinely cares for the school within his parish and is a regular visitor for assemblies and RE lessons. Sadly communication skills with young children are not his strength. Eventually the Headteacher plucks up courage and speaks to the Minister.

'You know that the children appreciate you coming in very much but we're finding some of your ideas go over their heads. Last week's thoughts on consubstantiation versus transubstantiation have left some of us very confused (and that's just the staff!). Could you perhaps try and be more child-centred in your approach?'

The Minister decides a fresh approach is called for and eagerly awaits his next opportunity to share his new perspectives with the children in an RE lesson.

'Good morning, children. Now, I want you to guess who I am. I'm grey, I have a bushy tail and I eat nuts. Who am I?'

The children, still recovering from last week's class discussion on the mysteries of the Incarnation, are for once lost for words.

'Come on, you must know! I'm grey, I have a bushy tail and I eat nuts. Who am I?'

Eventually one brave eight-year-old ventures a possible solution: 'Well, I know the answer should be Jesus but it sounds like a squirrel to me!'

The above story illustrates some of the false expectations children (and teachers) can have about assessment in RE. For many reasons teachers have sometimes shied away from any attempt at assessing pupils' learning in RE. It's therefore important to establish the key principles which govern RE and assessment. These are outlined on the following page. Nine sample assessment sheets are provided at the end of this chapter (pages 65–73).

If in RE we are encouraging a range of different learning and teaching strategies, it follows that assessment activities can be developed in a number of ways. Children can demonstrate progress in RE through the following means:

- *Written work* expressing their understanding of key beliefs and practices within religion. This could be done using a picture stimulus (see Assessment Sheets 1 and 2), or children could explore ideas and concepts through writing in the forms of stories, poems, diaries or use a word box (see Assessment Sheet 3) to develop their understanding.

GOOD ASSESSMENT IN RE

- Is part of the teaching and learning process and not an added extra bolted on at the end of the planning process.

- Balances the formative (what children already know and understand), the diagnostic (usually in a test form and indicating where children are failing to develop in their understanding) and the summative (the progress children have made in their knowledge, understanding, skills and attitudes).

- Has clear and achievable objectives which the children are aware of.

- Builds on previous learning and opens up new directions and developments.

- Involves children directly in their learning.

- Communicates clearly to other interested groups, such as parents, the progress children are making in RE.

- Recognizes that some aspects of RE (e.g. children's spiritual development and matters they wish to keep private) are not appropriate for formal assessment.

- Is concerned with making informed judgements from a clear evidence base. This involves the collation and use of different kinds of evidence (oral, written, creative and artistic expression) over a period of time.

- *Oral work* (individual, paired and/or group work) where children, through dialogue with their teacher, demonstrate their progress in learning (see Examples 1–3, pages 63–64).
- *Creative and expressive outcomes.* Children could demonstrate their understanding of religious beliefs and practices through role-play, dance and drama (e.g. the re-enactment of the story of the Prodigal Son could highlight themes of love and forgiveness). Children could also express their understanding through art, e.g. design a poster to highlight key beliefs in Islam. This could be followed by oral work in which children explain the reasons for choices within their artwork.

♦ Self-assessment

From the earliest age it is important to encourage children to evaluate their own learning in RE. Assessment Sheets 4 and 5 provide two examples of ways of helping children to assess their own progress in RE.

◆ Teacher-based Assessment

Obviously the teacher has a critical role in supporting children's progress in RE. Assessment Sheets 6–9 are formative and summative assessment grids on the Christian celebration of Christmas and the introduction of another world religion, namely Islam.

◆ Oral Assessment

Example 1
Key statement of attainment: Identify some religious stories and their possible meaning.

Children could:

- Listen to the story of the Prodigal Son.
- Discuss the feelings of the characters in the story.
- Discuss children's own experiences related to these feelings (jealousy, forgiveness, saying sorry, running away, not being very popular).
- Discuss some of the 'surprising' elements of the story, e.g. why is the father not cross with the son?
- Discuss what the story might be saying about the relationship between God and human beings according to Christian belief.
- Reflect quietly on a key question emerging from the story, e.g. 'Is it sometimes hard to say sorry?'

RE teachers should have the confidence to allow children to engage in stories at their own level of understanding rather than impose a 'definitive' meaning. For example, one eight-year-old responding to the question 'Who in the story [of the Good Samaritan] showed the greatest trust?' replied, 'The innkeeper. How did he know that the Samaritan would come back?' – the answer the teacher had anticipated being 'The Samaritan'.

Example 2
Key statement of attainment: Explain that some people act in particular ways because of their religious beliefs.

Using pictures, photographs, video and artefacts as an initial stimulus, children could discuss how special moments in life, like birth, are sometimes marked by a religious ceremony.

This could include children:

- Sharing their own experiences or those of family and friends in relation to welcoming a baby.
- Discussing their thoughts and feelings in relation to a new life, e.g. dependence, trust, care, noise!
- Discussing what makes ceremonies special, e.g. 'Where do they happen?' or 'Are special words used, such as promises?' or 'Who is involved in the ceremony and what are their roles?' or 'Are special clothes worn?'
- Reflecting upon a key aspect of welcoming a new life, e.g. 'What are the most important things a new baby needs?'

Children's oral work could then be reinforced through art, e.g. drawing special things involved in a religious ceremony, and/or writing, e.g. describing three important things which happen at a birth ceremony within the religion(s) being studied.

Example 3
Key statement of attainment: Explain that for some people religion is the most important thing for them.

Using the historical figure of Dr Barnardo as an example, children could:

- Talk about situations in which they have helped or have been helped by others.
- Discuss what makes some people want to help others.
- Explore the practical ways in which Dr Barnardo tried to put his Christian faith into action.
- Talk about the way Christians today try and help others, locally (e.g. a church community supporting a homelessness project) and/or globally (finding out about and discussing the work of Christian Aid, focusing on a specific project).
- Discuss the important beliefs and teachings which command/encourage Christians to care for others.
- Talk about key beliefs in another religion which focus on looking after others, e.g. the support through Zakah that Muslims provide.

Time to Think

1. What for you are the key issues in assessing RE?
2. How can you improve the assessment and reporting of RE in your school?

Christianity

Naomi has always wanted to know more about special objects found inside some churches. Can you help her understand some of these special objects?

This symbol is called a ....

It is special for Christians because

....

This type of cross is called a ....

It reminds Christians of when ....

....

The bird is an ....

The special object is a ....

and is used for ....

....

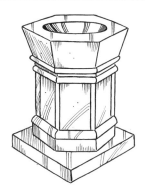

This object is often found at the church entrance. It is called a ....

and is used for ....

....

These two Christian symbols are

a .... and a ....

They are used as symbols because

....

Some churches have beautiful windows made from ....

What might you find in the picture?

....

Judaism

Joe's class have had a visitor from the Jewish community to talk about his special objects and why they are important to him. Can you recognize any and say what they might be used for?

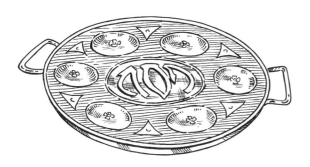

This special plate is called a ....
.... Jewish people use this
when they celebrate ....

This special cup is a .... cup.
It is used ....
....

This is a .... It is important
for Jews because ....
....

This is a .... It is used for
....
....

This is the .... On it is the
special Jewish symbol called ....
.... Next to it is a ....
This is used when people read from
the scroll because ....
....

Helping Hands

You might have heard people say, 'I know you like the back my hand.' Do you really know your own hands? Have a really close look at them. Perhaps there are lines and marks you've never noticed before.

Try drawing an outline of your hand on a piece of paper. Now put it on the floor with hand drawings from all the other children in your class. Can you still recognize your hand? Could you pick out your friend's hand?

In the box below you'll find some words which describe ways we can use our hands. Choose words from the box and put them in either the hand labelled 'Hands That Help' or the hand labelled 'Hands That Don't Help'. Two have been done for you.

care • push • pat • help • clench • smack • gentle • break • heal
stroke • hit • rough • safe • steal • give • snap • slap
explore • nip • tear • pinch • look after

Hands That Help   **Hands That Don't Help**

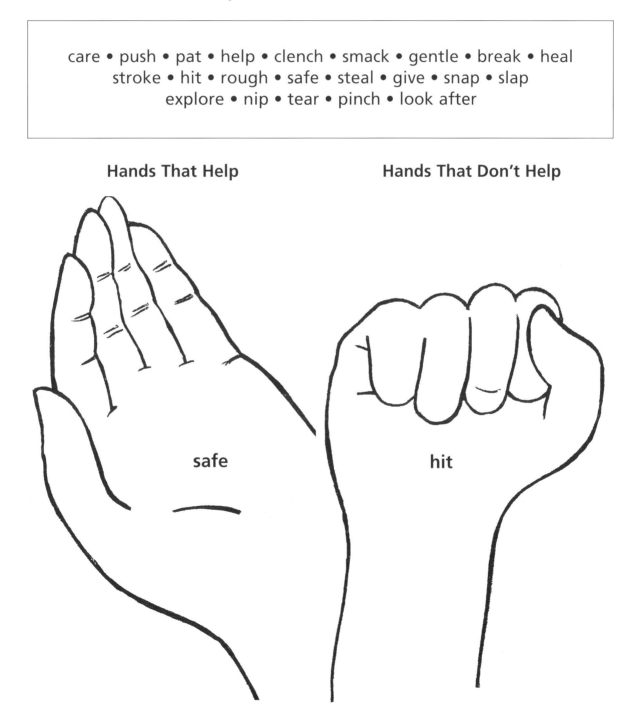

safe   hit

Self-Assessment

Topic review on

My name is

What I remember most from this topic is

Something I have learned is

As a result of doing this topic I'd like to find out more about

The best things I've done in this topic are

I can improve my work by

What I found hard was

Self-Assessment

My name

....

My class

....

It was easy to think about

....

....

....

....

....

....

I needed more help with

....

....

....

....

....

....

I found this topic

....

....

....

....

....

....

I was pleased with

....

....

....

....

....

....

It was difficult to

....

....

....

....

....

....

If I did this work again, these are the changes I would make:

....

....

....

....

....

Formative Assessment

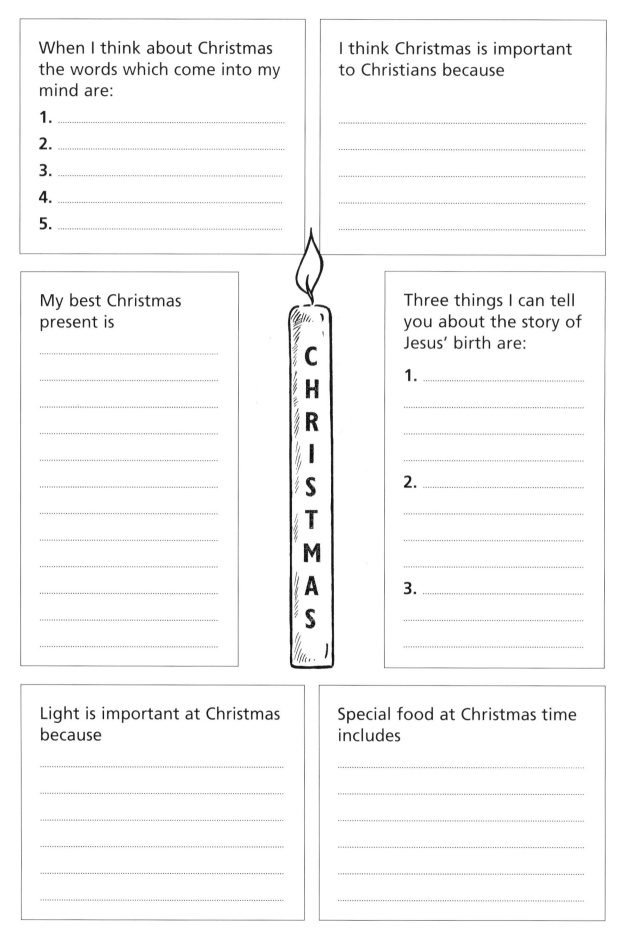

When I think about Christmas the words which come into my mind are:

1. ....
2. ....
3. ....
4. ....
5. ....

I think Christmas is important to Christians because

....
....
....
....
....

My best Christmas present is

....
....
....
....
....
....
....
....
....
....

Three things I can tell you about the story of Jesus' birth are:

1. ....
....
....

2. ....
....
....

3. ....
....

Light is important at Christmas because

....
....
....
....
....

Special food at Christmas time includes

....
....
....
....
....

Summative Assessment

Christmas is celebrated in different parts of the world by

....

....

....

....

....

....

I now know Christmas is important to Christians because

....

....

....

....

....

....

The star is important in the Christmas story because

....

....

....

....

....

....

....

....

....

....

This special Christian symbol is called a

....

The things on it represent

....

....

....

New things I have discovered about the story of the birth of Jesus are

....

....

....

....

....

The Christmas present I would like to give most is

....

because ....

....

....

Formative Assessment

The things I know about Islam are

_____

_____

_____

_____

_____

_____

The most important things I believe in are

_____

_____

_____

_____

_____

_____

A book that has helped me is

_____

because _____

_____

_____

_____

_____

A place I would really like to visit is

_____

because _____

_____

_____

_____

_____

Islam

Someone I'd like to help or something I'd like to help with is

_____

because _____

_____

_____

_____

A person I would like to meet is

_____

because _____

_____

_____

_____

Summative Assessment

Five important things Muslims believe are:

1. ....

....

2. ....

....

3. ....

....

4. ....

....

5. ....

....

The things I'd like to know about Islam are

....

....

....

....

....

....

....

....

....

In Islam, when a baby is born the first words they hear are

....

....

....

....

....

....

....

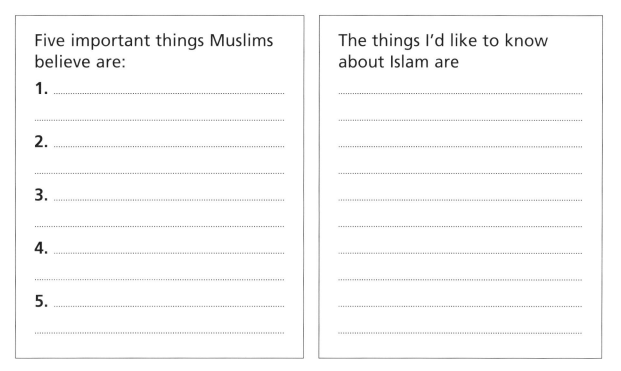

Islam

Makkah (Mecca) is important for Muslims because

....

....

....

....

....

....

....

....

These important Muslim words mean:

Imam ....

Mosque ....

Islam ....

Ka'bah ....

Qur'an ....

Ummah ....

Muslims help one another by

....

....

....

....

....

....

....

CHAPTER FIVE

Teaching Strategies in RE

The purpose of this chapter is to explore different ways of helping RE 'come alive' in the classroom. In Chapter 3 we considered the central issues which affect children's learning and the range of teaching strategies available for the RE teacher to develop. This chapter will take three key strategies – story, artefacts and reflective learning – and explain how they can be used effectively in the primary classroom.

Using Story in RE

Story has played a major part in RE (sometimes it appears to have been the only part) and used effectively it can be a powerful tool in developing children's knowledge and understanding. Stories have a natural place in children's (and adults') lives. The great strength of many stories, including those from religious traditions, is that they can be appreciated and interpreted at different levels, enabling children to explore themselves, their relationships, their environment and providing the opportunity to explore important questions. Stories can highlight the conflicts between good and evil, allow children to develop empathy with characters and feelings, help children to recognize both beauty and ugliness in the world and to explore issues and feelings which are beyond the ordinary and everyday.

One key factor is to allow children to respond to story at their own levels of insight and understanding and not to impose the 'correct' interpretation upon them. For example, a group of eight-year-olds were discussing the Garden of Eden aspect of the creation story in Genesis (chapters 2 and 3) and had been asked what in their opinion was the most important message of the story. Their answers reveal the different responses children can make to the same stimulus:

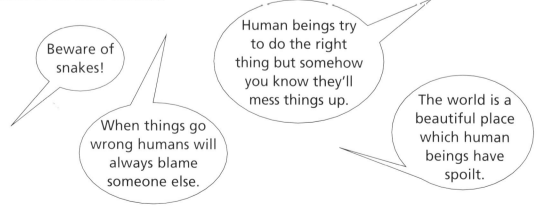

◆ Encouraging Responses

Children's response to story can be encouraged through:

- Asking questions about characters and events.
- Allowing the children to predict what may happen next.
- Helping them to comment on the way characters change and why.
- Asking them how the experiences and feelings of the characters relate to their own lives.
- Reflecting upon the meaning(s) of the story and how this relates to the questions the children themselves have raised about the story.
- A range of follow up activities including writing, dance/movement, role-play, drama and other forms of creative expression.

Within RE stories can cover a whole range of themes and activities. Some stories relate effectively to the 'implicit' aspect of RE, e.g. helping children explore feelings, relationships, values and their spiritual and moral development. Other stories can be drawn directly from religious traditions. In many faiths story has a significant place within religious belief and practice. While it is important to consider how sacred texts have significance for faith members (e.g. the authority of sacred texts and how they are handled and used in worship), it is also important to engage children directly in religious stories, and how they link to children's own lives and experiences.

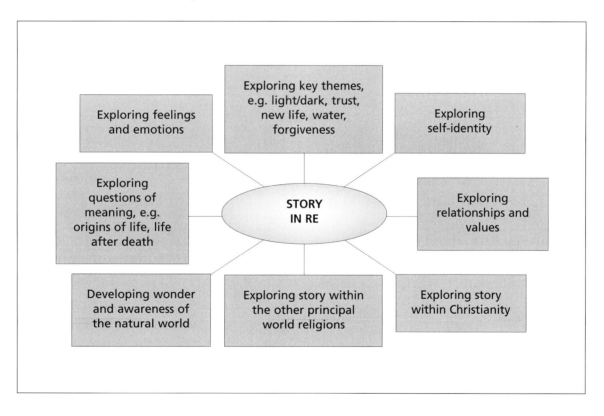

The following pages provide examples of how story could be used in the classroom. The four charts (pages 76–77) provide guidance on key elements in a story, mapping and presenting a story then providing follow-up activities. Next comes a planning sheet for exploring stories in RE (page 78). The remaining material on story (pages 79–83) looks at three specific stories and how they could be developed in the classroom.

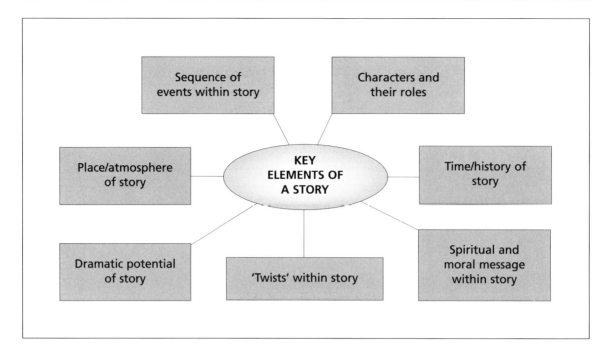

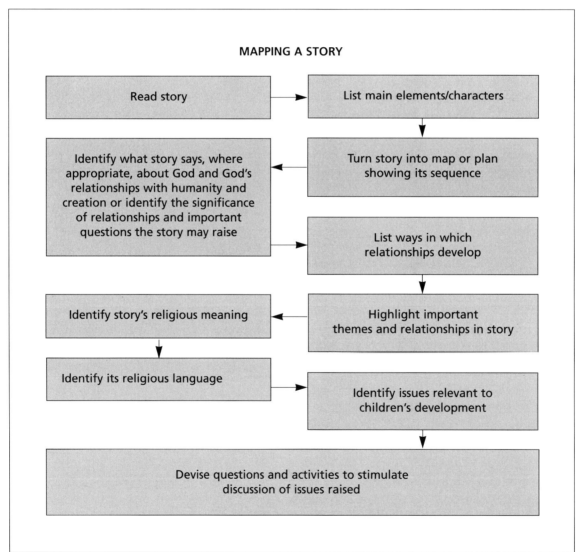

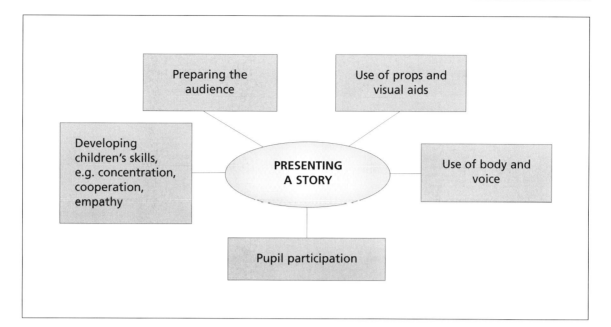

EXPLORING STORY: PLANNING SHEET

Title

Author

Publisher

RE-related themes

Outline of story

Key questions to address

Follow-up activities

EXPLORING STORY: EXAMPLE 1

Title The Whale's Tale

Author Jim Forest

Publisher Hunt & Thorpe

RE-related themes   * Obedience   * Sacrifice   * Faith

Outline of story

Humorous version of 'Jonah and the Whale' told from the whale's point of view. Whale introduces itself then relates the story, keeping close to the Bible version, but adding humorous modern language and fun.

Key questions to address

* What do children think Jonah was like? Brave? Resourceful? Disobedient? Self-willed?
* Why did Jonah end up in such a sticky situation?
* What would we do when faced with things we didn't want to do?
* Jonah thought God was telling him to do something. Who tells us to do things?

Follow-up activities

* Rewriting a different Bible story using modern-day language
* Writing about Jonah's thoughts and feelings when he was inside the whale
* Keeping and breaking rules: group and class discussion
* Picture strip of the story
* Collage of key events
* Drama day on the story *(see overleaf)*

RE and Drama

Jonah and the Whale

The following 'frames' provide a sequence of activities to use to tell the story of Jonah and the Whale. The idea is for groups of children to create the different frames or scenes. Each frame can be 'frozen' (i.e. the children within the scene stay completely still). The other children can then ask questions or say what they think is taking place in the frame. The full Bible version of this story can be found in chapters 1–3 of the Book of Jonah.

FRAME 1
MESSAGES

In pairs, children think about different ways of sending messages (e.g. phone, letter, morse code) and share these with the rest of the class.

FRAME 4
JONAH HEARS GOD'S MESSAGE AND RUNS AWAY

In groups, children create images and invent ideas on running away and hiding.

FRAME 3
THE NASTY PEOPLE OF NINEVEH

Children could make masks showing the nasty side of human nature (e.g. greed, cruelty).

FRAME 2
BUILDING A SHIP

In groups, children work together to build a ship (e.g. making carrying measuring, hammering movements).

FRAME 6
JONAH IS WOKEN TO PRAY FOR THE STORM TO END

Children create the scene, including Jonah asleep, drawing straws, a regretful Jonah.

FRAME 5
ON BOARD: THE STORM

In groups, children create storm sequences and express feelings of fear and panic.

FRAME 7
JONAH GOES OVERBOARD AND IS SWALLOWED BY THE WHALE

Children re-enact the scene, including the struggle to get the ship back to shore, the prayers for help, the throwing overboard of Jonah and the instant calming of the sea.

FRAME 8
JONAH INSIDE THE WHALE

Children reflect in movement Jonah's thoughts and feelings: fear, safety, confusion, sorrow, thankfulness.

FRAME 9
JONAH WARNS THE PEOPLE OF NINEVEH

Children 'hot seat' Jonah, asking questions about his experiences and message.

A range of follow-up activities, including collage work and reflecting on the meanings of the story, could be developed.

EXPLORING STORY: EXAMPLE 2

Title A Wonderful Hajj or What Should I Do?

Author Traditional Muslim story

Publisher A version of this story appears in 'RE Today' (Spring 1992), published by CEM (Christian Education Movement)

RE-related themes
* Friendship
* Companionship
* Support
* Belonging

Outline of story

A Muslim man, Ahmed, longs to go on Hajj. After many years of saving he is ready to go. As he is about to leave he meets his friend Mushaq, who has lost his job and has little food for his family. Ahmed does not go on Hajj but shares his money with Mushaq. Ahmed hears from his friends that Hajj has been very special. 'Was it wonderful?' Ahmed asks. 'Of course,' his friends reply, 'but you know it was, we saw you there.'

Key questions to address

* Is friendship most important of all?
* Should you follow rules blindly, or are there sometimes special circumstances?
* Would you have gone on the trip?
* If not, why not?
* What feelings might Ahmed and Mushaq have experienced in the story?

Follow-up activities

* Have you ever been kind or shared something?
* Story sequencing
* Travel preparations and journey plans
* Disappointments and ways of coping with them

EXPLORING STORY: EXAMPLE 3

Title Morning Beach

Author Leslie Baker

Publisher Little, Brown

RE-related themes   * Relationships   * Feelings/emotions   * Memories

Outline of story

Little girl goes on holiday with Mum to Grandma's and each year retraces a special trip to the sea. This year everything happens as usual, and she talks about feelings, reactions and memories as they cycle along the route until they discover the path is closed. Mother remembers alternative route which gives fresh experiences and eventually leads to their special beach.

Key questions to address

* Do you have any special thing you like to do with your parent(s)?
* Discuss the various feelings and emotions the girl experienced.
* When the path was closed did it spoil her trip?
* What other opportunities did it open up for her?

Follow-up activities

* Share your special times with a friend.
* Draw a special place for you.
* Find out more about special places and journeys within religion.

Using Artefacts in RE

♦ What Is an Artefact?

An artefact is something made by humans, generally for a particular purpose, e.g. a flower-pot. Religious artefacts are those objects which have a special, religious significance and purpose for believers within a faith tradition. In RE the definition is often widened to include certain naturally occurring items, such as the conch shells blown during Hindu worship.

♦ How and Why Can Artefacts be Used in RE?

- Artefacts can be used in the classroom as a stimulus for discussion, to arouse interest in religious traditions, for story-writing, drama work, art and technology.
- They can help answer questions raised by pupils such as 'How do Muslims pray?' or 'What is the Hindu puja tray?'
- They can be used for investigations in which pupils are finding out more about the origins, purpose and meanings associated with certain beliefs and practices of a faith tradition.
- They are invaluable for display and demonstration, illustrating how believers practise their traditions by showing exactly what is used.
- They can create a special mood, an atmosphere in the classroom, enabling pupils to develop a sense of faith traditions as living communities, perhaps giving an insight into the thoughts and feelings of a believer.
- Lastly, artefacts can be used not only to learn about religion, but to learn from religion. In the process of finding out more about the object, its origin, purpose and significance to believers, pupils can discover more about themselves by imagining and reflecting.

Through RE pupils should not just learn about religion but they should also learn about themselves from religion. (Michael Grimmitt)

Note that care and sensitivity need to be demonstrated when using religious artefacts in the classroom as they are precious and special for some people.

One approach to using artefacts, developed by the Religious Education Artefact Project at Birmingham University (REAP), takes pupils through different activities moving from learning about the religious artefact to personal reflection and learning from it. The first stage is engagement with and discovery of the artefact, by direct observation and questions, e.g. 'What can you see?' or 'What colour, size and shape is it?' One possible strategy at this stage is to explore the artefact using the five senses, since many artefacts relate to more than one, e.g. the Hindu puja (worship) tray. This can be particularly appropriate for younger children or those with special educational needs. (See also page 86.)

The second stage looks at the context from which the artefact originates. This requires research and information which may result in identification, ideas on what the artefact is used for and its significance for believers, e.g. 'This is a ... It is used for ...'.

Lastly, the reflection stage builds upon an understanding of the religious significance of the artefact and develops a personal meaning for the pupils in terms of reflective questions such as 'What do you do ...?' or 'Do you have ...?' For example, the mezuzah fastened to the doorpost of a Jewish home contains a text which reminds Jews of their beliefs, giving them guidance for living. Here, reflective questions such as 'What are your rules?' and 'Where do they come from?' or 'Who/what helps you to keep them?' could be asked. In this way, Religious Education can make a major contribution to pupils' spiritual and moral development.

Follow-up work can include the exploration of key religious concepts related to the artefact and how the artefact fits into the broader pattern of religious belief, practice and forms of expression.

A planning sheet illustrating this approach is provided on page 87, followed by four examples on using statues of the Buddha and St Francis of Assisi, a Torah mantle and a Hindu shrine.

Teachers interested in developing work with artefacts in the classroom are strongly recommended to read Christine Howard's book *Investigating Artefacts in Religious Education* (RMEP).

A wide range of artefacts for RE is available from:

Articles of Faith Ltd, REsource House, Kay Street, Bury BL9 6BU
(tel. 0161-7636232; fax. 0161-7633421).

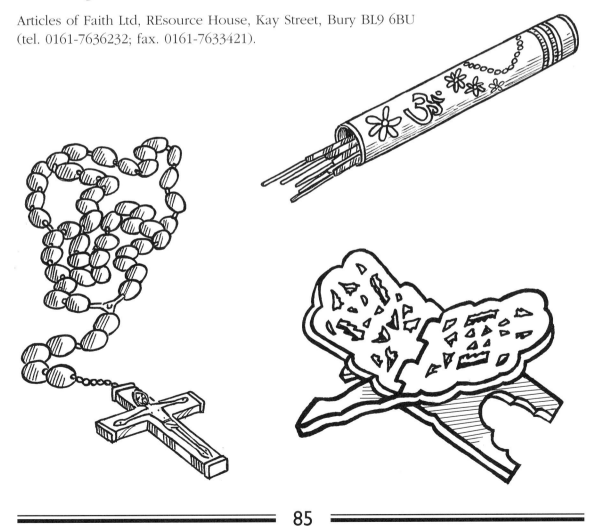

		EXPLORING ARTEFACTS THROUGH THE SENSES: SOME EXAMPLES				
	BUDDHISM	**CHRISTIANITY**	**HINDUISM***	**ISLAM**	**JUDAISM**	**SIKHISM**
SIGHT	Statue of Buddha	Paschal candle, icon or cross	Arti lamp	Qur'an – on reading stand	Shabbat or Hanukkah candles	Turban
HEARING	Ghanta (bell)	Church bell	Bell		Gregger (rattle)	
TASTE	Alms bowl	Bread and wine/ grape juice	Prashad		Seder plate/ meal	Karah parshad
TOUCH	Juzu beads (prayer-beads laid out 'to represent the human shape')	Rosary	Kum kum/ sandalwood paste	Prayer-beads	Mezuzah	Mala (prayer-beads) and kara (steel wristband)
SMELL	Incense	Incense	Incense	Perfume (alcohol-free)	Havdalah spice-box	

* All the items in the Hinduism column feature on a puja (worship) tray. The arti lamp is filled with ghee. The bell is rung at the beginning of puja. Prashad is food offered by devotees then consumed by them. Sandalwood is placed in a dish and used to mark the forehead of the devotee. Burning incense creates an aroma for the deity.

USING ARTEFACTS: PLANNING SHEET

Artefact

Religion

Stage 1. Engagement and Discovery – Key Questions

Stage 2. Context – Key Information

Stage 3. Reflection – Key Questions

Follow-up – Key Concepts

USING ARTEFACTS: EXAMPLE 1

Artefact Statue of Buddha

Religion Buddhism

Stage 1. Engagement and Discovery – Key Questions

What colour is it?
What do you think it is?
What shape is it?
What position are the hands in?

Stage 2. Context – Key Information

Story of Gotama Siddattha (Gautama Siddhartha)
Eightfold Path and Four Noble Truths

Stage 3. Reflection – Key Questions

What would you give up in life?
Who do you follow?
What do you think about when you are quiet?
What rules do you have for your life?

Follow-up – Key Concepts

Buddha, anicca, dukkha, kamma

USING ARTEFACTS: EXAMPLE 2

Artefact Statue of St Francis of Assisi

Religion Christianity

Stage 1. Engagement and Discovery – Key Questions

Can you tell me what kind of man this is?
What do you think his job is?
What is he wearing?
What is he holding?

Stage 2. Context – Key Information

Story of St Francis and the wolf and other animals
Can you think of another story with a dove in it?

Stage 3. Reflection – Key Questions

Who/what do you care for?
What would you give up for others?

Follow-up – Key Concepts

Sacrifice, obedience, commitment

USING ARTEFACTS: EXAMPLE 3

Artefact Torah mantle

Religion Judaism

Stage 1. Engagement and Discovery – Key Questions

What do you think this is made of?
What objects can you recognize?
What might it be used for?
Are there any symbols or words that you recognize?
Where do you think this might be kept?

Stage 2. Context – Key Information

Covers Torah scrolls, containing Jewish Law. Made of velvet decorated with several important Jewish symbols. Jews often call the Torah the crown of life. The lions (symbolizing power and strength) are guarding two tablets bearing the first words in Hebrew of the Ten Commandments.

Stage 3. Reflection – Key Questions

What are your most important rules?
Have you always kept them?

Follow-up – Key Concepts

Torah, teshuva, mitzvah

USING ARTEFACTS: EXAMPLE 4

Artefact Hindu shrine with images of Shiva and Parvati

Religion Hinduism

Stage 1. Engagement and Discovery – Key Questions

What do you think this is?
Why is it so brightly coloured?
Why are there bells hanging from the roof?
Do you think the two people inside are special? Why?

Stage 2. Context – Key Information

Shiva is one of the most important of all the Hindu ideas of God. Holds a trident representing three parts of his character. Many Hindus think of Shiva as the destroyer of life but he does not destroy for no reason but so that life can begin again, just as a flower must die so that new seeds can be sown. Snake next to trident is another way of recognizing Shiva: shows that he has the power to deal with and conquer death.

Parvati, Shiva's wife, is a gentle, mild figure. Many Hindu women wear a red mark on their own foreheads like the one on hers.

This shrine is similar to those used by Hindus in their own homes for worship and contains many features of a Hindu temple. Bells are rung to attract attention of god or goddess. Four pillars and fence show that area where Shiva and Parvati are is special (holy) and different from outside world. Roof shaped like mountain to show Shiva's importance and strength. Bright colours used so that worshippers' attention is quickly drawn to shrine.

Stage 3. Reflection – Key Questions

Do you have a special place? What is it like?

Follow-up – Key Concepts

Ahimsa, avatar, samsara

A Time to Be Still

'Be still and know'

Within many religious traditions, important moments of revelation have taken place not against a background of noise and bustle, but at moments of peace and calm. It is really helpful likewise for children (and teachers) to have opportunities to be still and reflective, especially during busy and active days at school.

It would be easy to be sceptical about the notion of asking some children to be still, even if for only a few seconds! However, just as children need to practise certain skills when learning a new sport, so too, in terms of their spiritual development, they need practice at effectively using stillness and quiet thought.

Developing children's reflective skills in RE supports children's learning across the curriculum by:

- Improving concentration and self-discipline.
- Developing the ability to find and creatively use inner quietness.
- Highlighting the importance of their thoughts and feelings.
- Developing their imaginative and creative potential and effective use of all their senses.
- Enabling them to see that some special moments of learning take place when we are still and quiet.
- Encouraging them to use quiet reflection during lessons.
- Improving their well-being and ability to relax.

◆ Getting Started – Some Ideas for the Classroom

When introducing or developing reflective activities like those suggested in this section, teachers should note the following key points:

- The teacher's role is essential in creating an appropriate learning environment. The voice needs to be calm and measured and children's feelings and responses need to be valued. There also needs to be a time for sharing and responding to the activities undertaken. Follow-up work can take the form of discussion, creative writing, drama or artistic responses.

- Some children may initially feel inhibited and uncomfortable about stillness and reflection. It is important to point out that children don't have to take part in the activities but they don't have the right to disturb other children. In my experience children's initial reluctance is quickly overcome, particularly when they see the benefits of a reflective approach for other children.

- For effective reflective learning to take place the learning environment needs to be supportive. This means children valuing and respecting the activities, having enough room for children to sit and/or lie in comfort, using displays and music which enhance a sense of calm and stillness. It also means an atmosphere of encouragement and sensitivity, free of pressure.

Children are often unfamiliar with stillness and quiet so it is important to ease them into the learning techniques. To begin with the teacher could simply say to the class, 'Close your eyes and be still just for a few seconds. When you think 20 seconds have passed raise your hand.' (It is remarkable how long/short some children think that time interval is.)

Activity 1: Listening

TEACHER   Please make sure that you are sitting comfortably in your chair. I would like you to gently close your eyes so that you are not distracted by anyone. I would like you to listen very carefully to any sounds you can hear outside this room. They have been here while we have been working but perhaps we didn't really hear them. What different sounds can you hear? *(Pause for a few seconds.)*

I would now like us to listen to a different sound. Can you hear any sounds inside this room? What are they? Are they loud or quiet?' *(Pause for a few seconds.)*

I would now like you to listen to a very special sound ... a sound that's inside you ... the sound of your own breathing. Listen carefully to your own breath as it flows in and out. *(Pause for a few seconds.)*

Now, when you are ready, let's slowly open our eyes and come back together as a class.

Activity 2: Relaxing

TEACHER   I would like you to sit *(or lie on the floor, space and carpeting permitting)* comfortably. When you're ready it might help to close your eyes so that you are not distracted. *(If some children do not wish to close their eyes, encourage them to look at the floor rather than other children.)*

We're going to try and relax our bodies. First of all tighten your toes as though you were digging them into your feet ... hold this for a few moments ... now let go. Push your feet as hard as you can into the floor ... really push them ... now, let them relax. Tighten your calf muscles ... feel how tense they are ... let them relax. Now try the same with your thigh muscles ... feel the muscles slowly relaxing. Now we're going to move to our tummies. Imagine someone has just tried to hit you in the tummy and you've pulled it right back ... hold this for a few moments ... and now relax. Try the same with your shoulders ... squeeze them together as tightly as you can ... then relax. Next we're going to relax our hands. Make a fist shape and clench it as tightly as you can ... imagine you have something precious in your hand which someone else wants to take ... now let your fingers slowly uncurl and your hand relax. Now try and tighten the muscles in your neck ... squeeze them really tight ... then let go. Finally tighten the muscles in your face ... push them as hard as you can ... and now relax. Take a few deep breaths and when you're ready open your eyes and come back together as a group in this room.

Activity 3: Focusing on Objects

TEACHER I would like you to have a really good look round our classroom. *(Encourage children to walk round the room.)* We spend a lot of our day in here, but perhaps there are things that you've not noticed before. I'd like you now to choose one object in the room. Have a really good look at it ... What kind of shape is it? What does it feel like to touch? What colours can you see? ... I'd now like you to choose three words which describe your object ... don't say what it is but think about some words which tell you something about the object. I'd like you now to sit back in your place and share with a friend the words you've chosen ... see if they can guess the object you've been thinking about.

Activity 4: Focusing on a Special Place

TEACHER I would like you to slowly close your eyes ... we're going to be thinking about a special place. Just for a moment try and picture your favourite place ... Where is it? ... Are you on your own or with other people? ... Is it busy and noisy or quiet and still? What is it about this place which is special for you?

I would like to take you on a short journey to a beautiful place ... you're sitting on a quiet, peaceful beach. It is a lovely warm, sunny day. You can feel the warmth of the sun on your back and a gentle breeze from the sea ... you sit quietly down at the edge of the water. What can you see around you? What sounds can you hear?

You stay here just a few minutes enjoying the warmth and the stillness, watching the light on the water. It is a calm and special place ... Just picture the scene in your mind ... so that you can recall it whenever you want to.

Now it is time to leave the beach and come back to our classroom. Breathe a little more deeply to refresh your lungs and when you are ready open your eyes.

Activity 5. Exploring a Religious Dimension: Prayer

TEACHER I would like you to sit quietly and think about someone or something which is special for you. It might be a friend ... or a member of your family ... or something very special that you're really glad you have ... Just picture this person or object in your mind ... someone or something you are thankful for.

Now I'd like you to focus on something about yourself that you would like to change. Not about the way you look but something about you as a person ... perhaps you get cross easily ... or you would like to be more caring ... Just think for a few moments about what it is about yourself that you would like to change.

Now we are going to think about a person or a situation that needs help ... it might be a friend or something you've seen on the television ... Just picture in your mind this person or situation.

Finally I would like you to think about what you can do yourself to help this person or situation. How can you show you care about them or the situation? Just think quietly for a few seconds ... Now when you're ready let's come back together in our classroom.

Follow-up activity Children could divide a sheet of paper into four and draw/write about the following:

- Saying thank you for friends and special things.
- Saying sorry and wanting to change.
- Thinking about other people and situations.
- Reflecting on a practical response to other people/situations.

This activity can then be linked to different aspects of prayer (adoration and thanksgiving, confession and supplication), helping children to recognize that prayer is important within most religions and can have different modes of expression.

Time to Think

1. How you could introduce/develop times for reflection in your classroom?
2. How important is it for children to experience stillness and quiet thought?

Note Teachers interested in developing further the reflective aspect of RE are encouraged to use Mary Stone's book *Don't Just Do Something, Sit There* (RMEP).

CHAPTER SIX

In the Classroom

Christianity and the Other Principal Religions

♦ Exploring Christianity

Christianity is for some teachers the most difficult religion to teach, partly because of its influence in shaping Western society and partly because of the diversity in how Christianity is practised across the world. The diagram opposite sets out some starting-points for exploring key aspects of Christianity in the classroom. Before beginning to develop a teaching programme and detailed schemes of work on Christianity, it is also worth considering the following important principles:

- Christianity is a living and varied world-wide faith. There are millions of Christians and Christianity is growing numerically in different parts of the world.

- Christians enjoy worshipping God in different ways. Their practice varies from the creative use of silence and stillness in the monastic and Quaker traditions to the exuberant use of music and dancing in the Pentecostal tradition. It is important to help children recognize that Christians celebrate their faith through various styles of worship using different activities (e.g. dance, drama) and forms of music.

- Christians believe that their lives should be based on two specific commandments: 'Love the Lord your God with all your heart, with all your soul and with all your mind' and 'Love your neighbour as yourself' (Matthew 22:37–39). These beliefs have led and still lead many Christians into caring social action.

- Christianity is a monotheistic religion with a distinctive Trinitarian belief. Christians believe in one God who is all knowing and all powerful, the Creator of all things. This God can be known in three ways: as God the Father, God the Son (Jesus Christ) and God the Holy Spirit.

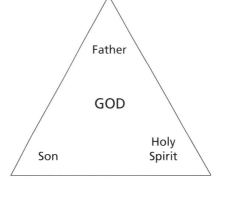

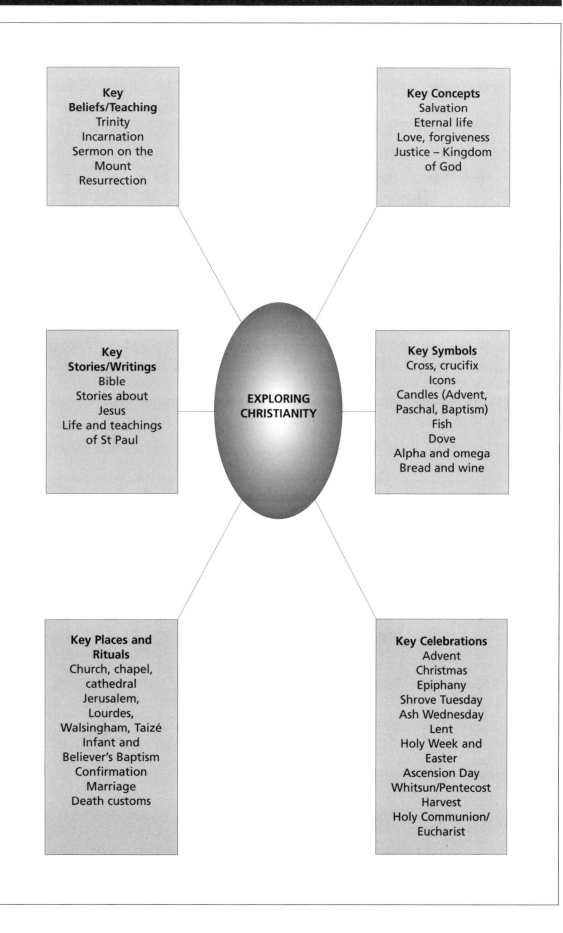

Key Beliefs/Teaching
Trinity
Incarnation
Sermon on the Mount
Resurrection

Key Concepts
Salvation
Eternal life
Love, forgiveness
Justice – Kingdom of God

Key Stories/Writings
Bible
Stories about Jesus
Life and teachings of St Paul

EXPLORING CHRISTIANITY

Key Symbols
Cross, crucifix
Icons
Candles (Advent, Paschal, Baptism)
Fish
Dove
Alpha and omega
Bread and wine

Key Places and Rituals
Church, chapel, cathedral
Jerusalem, Lourdes, Walsingham, Taizé
Infant and Believer's Baptism
Confirmation
Marriage
Death customs

Key Celebrations
Advent
Christmas
Epiphany
Shrove Tuesday
Ash Wednesday
Lent
Holy Week and Easter
Ascension Day
Whitsun/Pentecost
Harvest
Holy Communion/Eucharist

◆ Exploring the Other Principal Religions

One of the concerns some teachers have about RE is how to approach the teaching of world religions about which they themselves lack knowledge or understanding. This is sometimes compounded by the approach used in RE to the other principal religions. We have already seen in Chapter 3 that there is comparatively little attention given to other religions in Key Stages 1 and 2, with most of the emphasis being on celebration and festivals within a religious tradition.

There are many advantages for schools in using a thematic approach to RE, but without careful planning, this can lead to a superficial understanding of the world of religion. Suppose, for example, that a school uses the theme 'Light' in Year 2 and looks at Hanukkah and Divali. This may develop children's understanding of the concept of light but how far will it enhance their understanding of Judaism and Hinduism? If these festivals are all children learn about then there are huge areas of belief and practice which are not being explored. It is quite likely that children encountering Divali will themselves raise all kinds of questions such as 'Do Hindus have other special stories?' or 'What do Hindus believe?' or 'Do Hindus enjoy other celebrations?' This will then provide the opportunity for children to learn about Hindu beliefs, explore other Hindu stories (e.g. stories about Krishna) and find out about other Hindu celebrations (e.g. Holi). Good RE balances the thematic and systematic approaches so that children develop in their knowledge and understanding of religions, in their understanding of the theme being covered and how this relates to their own thoughts, feelings and experiences.

The diagrams on pages 99–103 are designed to provide a framework for exploring each of the five principal world religions in the classroom. Of course it will be impossible to cover all aspects of an individual religion, but the frameworks suggest possible starting-points for exploring key aspects of each religion.

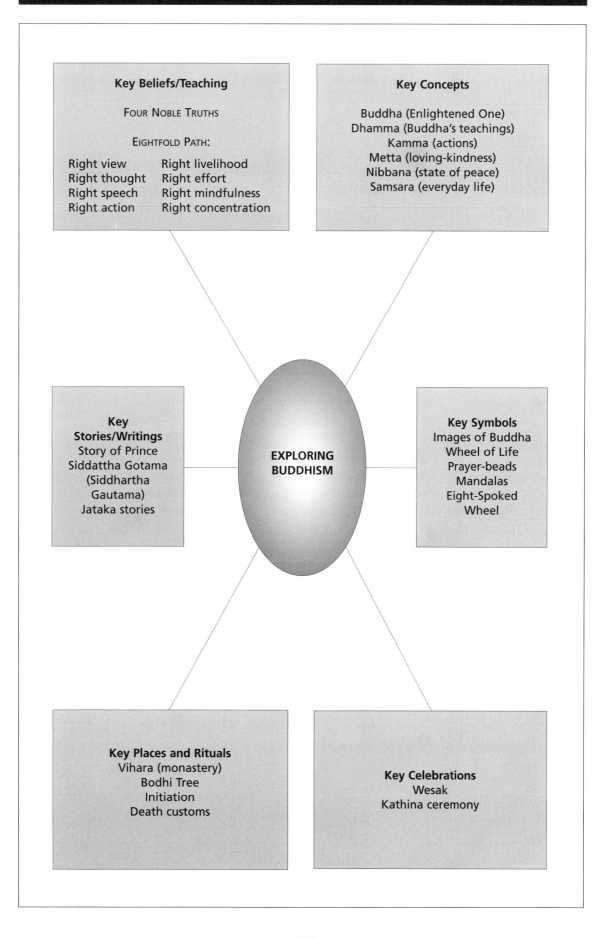

Key Beliefs/Teaching

FOUR NOBLE TRUTHS

EIGHTFOLD PATH:

Right view   Right livelihood
Right thought   Right effort
Right speech   Right mindfulness
Right action   Right concentration

Key Concepts

Buddha (Enlightened One)
Dhamma (Buddha's teachings)
Kamma (actions)
Metta (loving-kindness)
Nibbana (state of peace)
Samsara (everyday life)

Key Stories/Writings
Story of Prince Siddattha Gotama (Siddhartha Gautama)
Jataka stories

EXPLORING BUDDHISM

Key Symbols
Images of Buddha
Wheel of Life
Prayer-beads
Mandalas
Eight-Spoked Wheel

Key Places and Rituals
Vihara (monastery)
Bodhi Tree
Initiation
Death customs

Key Celebrations
Wesak
Kathina ceremony

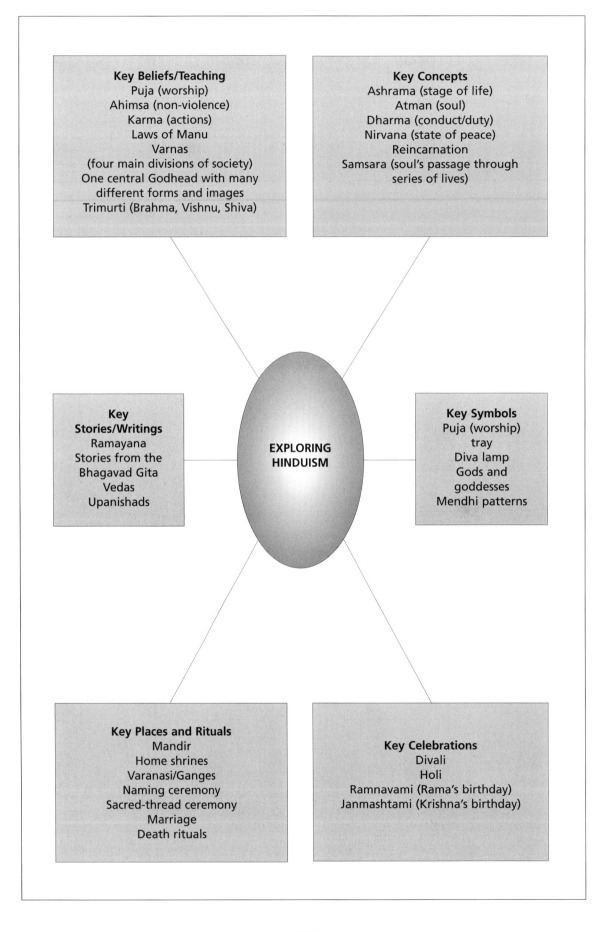

Key Beliefs/Teaching
Puja (worship)
Ahimsa (non-violence)
Karma (actions)
Laws of Manu
Varnas
(four main divisions of society)
One central Godhead with many
different forms and images
Trimurti (Brahma, Vishnu, Shiva)

Key Concepts
Ashrama (stage of life)
Atman (soul)
Dharma (conduct/duty)
Nirvana (state of peace)
Reincarnation
Samsara (soul's passage through
series of lives)

**Key
Stories/Writings**
Ramayana
Stories from the
Bhagavad Gita
Vedas
Upanishads

**EXPLORING
HINDUISM**

Key Symbols
Puja (worship)
tray
Diva lamp
Gods and
goddesses
Mendhi patterns

Key Places and Rituals
Mandir
Home shrines
Varanasi/Ganges
Naming ceremony
Sacred-thread ceremony
Marriage
Death rituals

Key Celebrations
Divali
Holi
Ramnavami (Rama's birthday)
Janmashtami (Krishna's birthday)

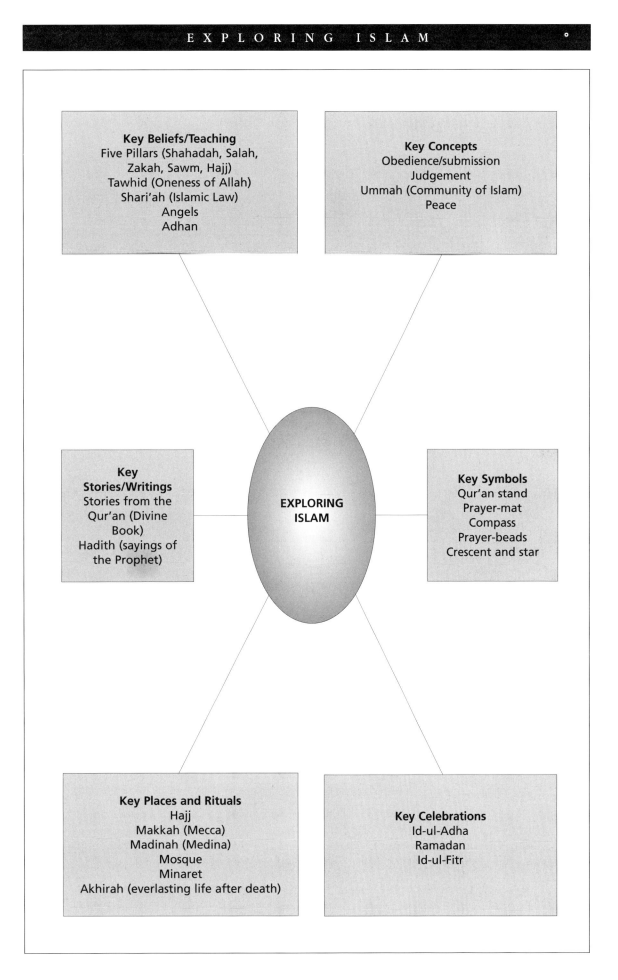

Key Beliefs/Teaching
Five Pillars (Shahadah, Salah,
Zakah, Sawm, Hajj)
Tawhid (Oneness of Allah)
Shari'ah (Islamic Law)
Angels
Adhan

Key Concepts
Obedience/submission
Judgement
Ummah (Community of Islam)
Peace

**Key
Stories/Writings**
Stories from the
Qur'an (Divine
Book)
Hadith (sayings of
the Prophet)

**EXPLORING
ISLAM**

Key Symbols
Qur'an stand
Prayer-mat
Compass
Prayer-beads
Crescent and star

Key Places and Rituals
Hajj
Makkah (Mecca)
Madinah (Medina)
Mosque
Minaret
Akhirah (everlasting life after death)

Key Celebrations
Id-ul-Adha
Ramadan
Id-ul-Fitr

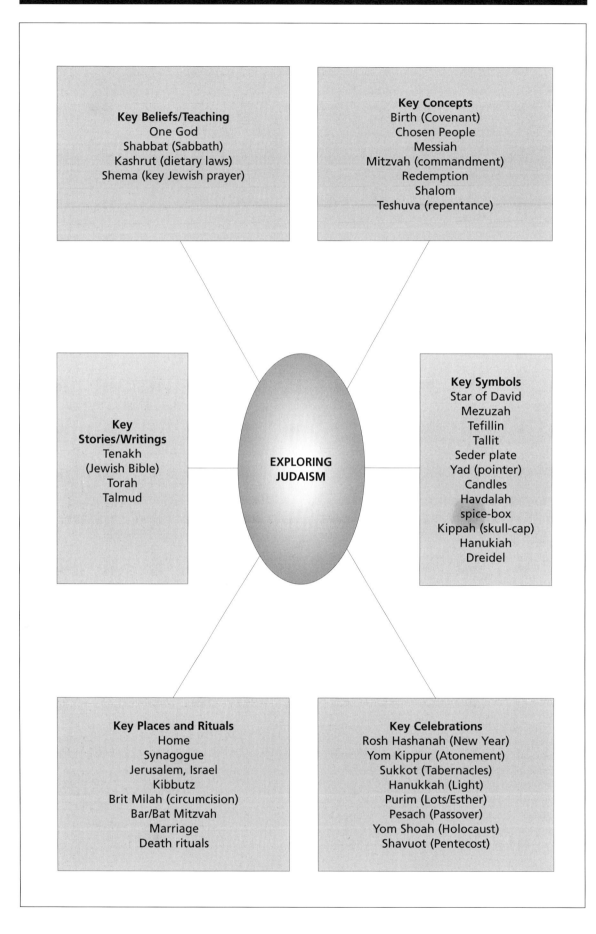

Key Beliefs/Teaching
One God
Shabbat (Sabbath)
Kashrut (dietary laws)
Shema (key Jewish prayer)

Key Concepts
Birth (Covenant)
Chosen People
Messiah
Mitzvah (commandment)
Redemption
Shalom
Teshuva (repentance)

Key Stories/Writings
Tenakh (Jewish Bible)
Torah
Talmud

EXPLORING JUDAISM

Key Symbols
Star of David
Mezuzah
Tefillin
Tallit
Seder plate
Yad (pointer)
Candles
Havdalah spice-box
Kippah (skull-cap)
Hanukiah
Dreidel

Key Places and Rituals
Home
Synagogue
Jerusalem, Israel
Kibbutz
Brit Milah (circumcision)
Bar/Bat Mitzvah
Marriage
Death rituals

Key Celebrations
Rosh Hashanah (New Year)
Yom Kippur (Atonement)
Sukkot (Tabernacles)
Hanukkah (Light)
Purim (Lots/Esther)
Pesach (Passover)
Yom Shoah (Holocaust)
Shavuot (Pentecost)

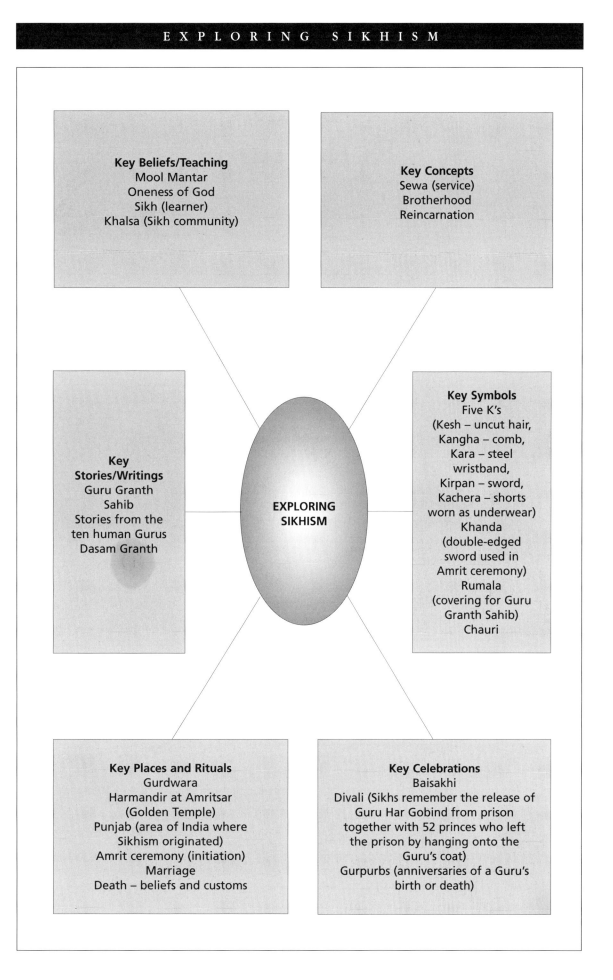

Key Beliefs/Teaching
Mool Mantar
Oneness of God
Sikh (learner)
Khalsa (Sikh community)

Key Concepts
Sewa (service)
Brotherhood
Reincarnation

Key Stories/Writings
Guru Granth Sahib
Stories from the ten human Gurus
Dasam Granth

EXPLORING SIKHISM

Key Symbols
Five K's
(Kesh – uncut hair,
Kangha – comb,
Kara – steel
wristband,
Kirpan – sword,
Kachera – shorts
worn as underwear)
Khanda
(double-edged
sword used in
Amrit ceremony)
Rumala
(covering for Guru
Granth Sahib)
Chauri

Key Places and Rituals
Gurdwara
Harmandir at Amritsar
(Golden Temple)
Punjab (area of India where
Sikhism originated)
Amrit ceremony (initiation)
Marriage
Death – beliefs and customs

Key Celebrations
Baisakhi
Divali (Sikhs remember the release of
Guru Har Gobind from prison
together with 52 princes who left
the prison by hanging onto the
Guru's coat)
Gurpurbs (anniversaries of a Guru's
birth or death)

Final
Reflections

Are You REady? has been written to help busy teachers feel more confident about effective planning and delivery in Religious Education. It has tried to emphasize the contribution RE can make to children's learning, especially in terms of their spiritual awareness. It has also sought to reassure teachers that there is nothing strange or 'weird' about contemporary RE that should make teachers feel threatened or uncomfortable about teaching it.

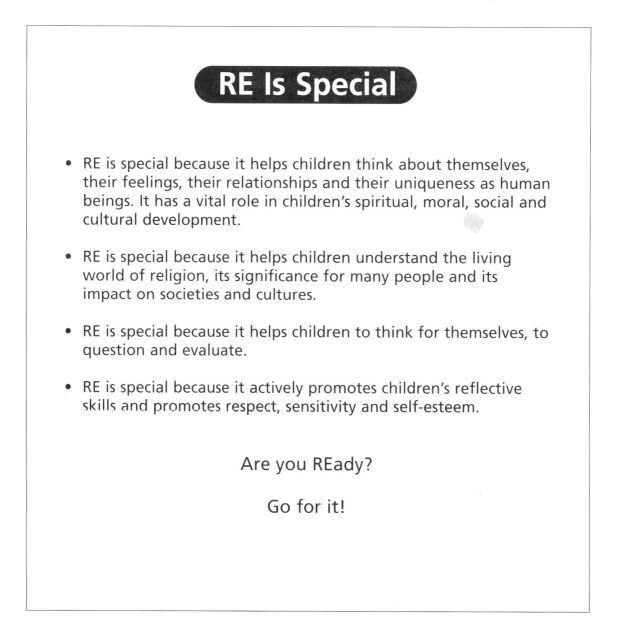

RE Is Special

- RE is special because it helps children think about themselves, their feelings, their relationships and their uniqueness as human beings. It has a vital role in children's spiritual, moral, social and cultural development.

- RE is special because it helps children understand the living world of religion, its significance for many people and its impact on societies and cultures.

- RE is special because it helps children to think for themselves, to question and evaluate.

- RE is special because it actively promotes children's reflective skills and promotes respect, sensitivity and self-esteem.

Are you REady?

Go for it!